Bryn Mawr Latin Commentaries

Minor Authors of the Corpus Tibullianum

John Yardley

Thomas Library
Bryn Mawr College
Bryn Mawr, Pennsylvania

Bryn Mawr Latin Commentaries

Editors

Julia Haig Gaisser   James J. O'Donnell

Bryn Mawr College   *University of Pennsylvania*

The purpose of the Bryn Mawr Latin Commentaries is to make a wide range of classical and post-classical authors accessible to the intermediate student. Each commentary provides the minimum grammatical and lexical information necessary for a first reading of the text.

The Bryn Mawr Latin Commentaries are supported by a generous grant from the Division of Education Programs of the National Endowment for the Humanities

Copyright ©1992 by Bryn Mawr College

Manufactured in the United States of America
ISBN 0-929524-74-8

Printed and distributed by
Bryn Mawr Commentaries
Thomas Library
Bryn Mawr College
Bryn Mawr, PA 19010

THE MINOR AUTHORS OF THE CORPUS TIBULLIANUM

The manuscripts of the *Corpus Tibullianum* contain three books, only the first two of which, it is now generally agreed, are the work of Tibullus. The third (which 15th century Italian scholars divided into two) is commonly believed to be a collection of elegies by various poets belonging to the literary circle to which Tibullus himself (and his younger contemporary Ovid) belonged. This is the circle of one of the two great literary patrons of the Augustan period, Marcus Valerius Messalla Corvinus (the other great patron, to whose circle Virgil, Horace and Propertius belonged, was Gaius Maecenas). The third book of the Corpus contains 20 poems, 19 of which appear in this edition; only the long poem known as the Panegyric of Messalla (*Panegyricus Messallae*) has been omitted.

The first six elegies of Book 3 (and of this edition) are by a poet who calls himself Lygdamus, evidently a pseudonym. He has been identified with various historical figures, including Ovid (on the basis of Lygdamus 5.18) and Tibullus himself, but no identification is compelling. The poems are addressed to his beloved Neaera, whose identity is likewise unknown, and employ many motifs, ideas and topoi common to the great elegists Propertius, Tibullus and Ovid.

After Lygdamus comes the *Panegyricus Messallae*, a poem in praise of the great patron, omitted from this edition. It is followed by five shorter elegies, known as the *The Garland of Sulpicia* (Section 2 in this edition, and throughout referred to as "Garland"). The poems, all thematically and stylistically in the tradition of Roman Love Elegy, deal with the love of Sulpicia, daughter of one Servius Sulpicius Rufus, and relative and (after her father's death) ward of Messalla, for a young man whom she calls Cerinthus, which is probably a pseudonym. Two are written in the person of Sulpicia (Garland 2 and 4), and the others in the person of the poet who, as an outsider, observes the love-affair of Sulpicia and Cerinthus. Many have ascribed the poems to Tibullus, but the evidence for this is weak.

After the Garland come six short elegies (a total of 40 lines), purportedly by Sulpicia herself (in this edition Section 3, "Sulpicia"). These are all concerned with her love for Cerinthus, and four of them (Sulpicia 3-6) are directly addressed to him.

Finally (Section 4 in this edition) there are two elegies by another unknown author which, once more, have often been attributed to Tibullus himself, because the author gives himself that name ("Two Poems" 2.13). Again arguments for their authenticity are not conclusive.

SELECT BIBLIOGRAPHY

Note: The text is that of J. P. Postgate's Oxford Classical Text (2nd ed. 1915). Grammatical references are to E. C. Woodcock *A New Latin Syntax* (London, 1959) and the Oxford Latin Dictionary (OLD).

Editions:

The Elegies of Albius Tibullus: The Corpus Tibullianum edited with
 introduction and Notes on Books I, II and IV, 2-14, by Kirby Flower
 Smith (reprinted Darmstadt, 1964). (Omits Lygdamus)
Albii Tibulli Carmina: Accedunt Sulpiciae Elegidia.
 Ed. Geyza Némethy (Budapest, 1905). (Omits Lygdamus)
Tibulle et les Auteurs du Corpus Tibullianum.
 Ed. A. Cartault (Paris, 1909).
Tibulle et les Auteurs du Corpus Tibullianum.
 Ed. L. Pichard (Paris, 1924).
Appendix Tibulliana.
 Ed. Hermann Tränkle (Berlin, 1990).

Translations:

J. P. Postgate in *Catullus, Tibullus and Pervigilium Veneris* (Loeb
 Classical Library: Cambridge, Mass. Revised and Reprinted 1924)
 pp. 287-339.
Philip Dunlop, *Tibullus: Poems* (Penguin: Harmondsworth 1972) pp.
 117-155.

Other:

Esther Bréguet, *Le Roman de Sulpicia: Elégies IV, 2-12 du Corpus
 Tibullianum* (Rome, 1972).
Ceri Davies, "Poetry in the 'Circle' of Messalla" *G & R* 20 (1973) 23-35.
Id., "The Elegies of Lygdamus: some considerations" *Trivium*
 1974, 26-38.
N. J. Lowe, "Sulpicia's Syntax" *CQ* N.S. 38 (1988) 193-205.
G. Luck, *The Latin Love Elegy*. (London: 2nd ed. 1969)
 Chapter 6 "Minor Talents."
Matthew S. Santirocco, "Sulpicia Reconsidered" *CJ* 74 (1979) 229-39.

METRICAL INTRODUCTION

Quantitative metre is based on various patterns of long (-) and short (u) syllables. Strictly speaking, one should know the quantity of a syllable (that is, whether it is long or short) by knowing whether the vowel in that syllable is naturally (i.e. is pronounced as) a long or a short; e.g. hĭc, "this", and the first vowel in mănĕo, "I stay", are naturally short, whereas hīc, "here", and the first vowel in māne, "in the morning" are naturally long.

However, a number of factors will help the student towards the metrical analysis (or "scansion") of a line, even if he/she is unsure of vowel-quantities:

1. A syllable, even if its vowel is naturally short, will be lengthened if followed by two or more consonants, whether or not those consonants are in the same word: e.g., primūs caram (Lygdamus 2.1) iuuenēm ferreus (Lygdamus 2.2).

    Note:
    a. Exceptions are when a vowel is followed by a "mute" (b, p, d, t, g or c) plus a "liquid" (l or r). So pătres or pātres.
    b. Letters "made up" of two consonants (x = cs; z = ts) count as two consonants. So felix, rixa.
    c. i may be a vowel (felix, hic) but sometimes it is a consonant (iam, iubeo).
    d. qu counts as a single consonant (Lygdamus 1.3 undīque pompa).

2. Diphthongs (e.g., ae, oe) are naturally long if they are pronounced as a single vowel (e.g. filiāe mōenia, fōedus).

3. A word ending with a vowel or m "elides", or "runs into", a following word beginning with a vowel: e.g., Lygdamus 1.9 lutea sed nive(um) inuoluat. But if the second word is es or est, its e is suppressed (prodelision): e.g., Lygdamus 1.19, mutua cura (e)st

4. h is not pronounced and so is ignored in scansion.

The Elegiac Couplet

The authors of the poems in the Tibullan corpus are all elegists, that is to say they write in elegiac couplets, the standard metre for Latin love poetry. The elegiac couplet is made up of a hexameter, a six-foot line, followed by a pentameter, regarded as a five-foot line.

In the hexameter, the foot may be one of two kinds: a spondee, i.e., two long syllables (- -), or a dactyl, i.e., a long syllable followed by two short syllables (- ∪∪). The fifth foot is almost always a dactyl, and the sixth is invariably a spondee (or a long followed by a short, which is said to be "lengthened by position"). The first four feet may be any combination of dactyls and spondees. Students first approaching elegy may find it easiest to "mark off" the fifth-foot dactyl and sixth-foot spondee before commencing the scansion of the rest of the line.

The *caesura* is a break between words within the metrical foot. So a hexameter may have several *caesurae*, but there will also be a main or central *caesura* (marked ^), usually in the third foot. So line 1 of Lygdamus is scanned as follows:

Mārtîs Rōmānî ^ fēstāē vĕnĕrĕ̆ kălēndāē

The pentameter, which is also composed of dactyls and spondees, falls into two halves of 2 1/2 feet separated by a word break (*diaeresis*) The first two feet may be either dactyls or spondees, but the rest of the line is invariably - || - ∪∪ |- ∪∪ | -, i.e., two dactyls preceded and followed by the two half-feet which, as it were, make up a spondee. So line 2 of Lygdamus is scanned:

ēxŏrīēns nōstrîs || hîc fŭĭt ānnŭs ăvîs.

Again students might be advised to work from the end of the line, filling in the long, dactyl, dactyl, long, before determining the nature of the two remaining feet.

Sulpicia 4 is scanned thus:

```
      - -    | - -| -    - | -    - | -  ∪∪ |-  -
   gratum (e)st, securus^multum quod iam tibi de me
```

```
           - -| -   ∪ ∪|- ||-    ∪   ∪| - ∪  ∪ | -
         permittis, subito ne mal(e) inepta cadam.
```

```
    - ∪ ∪| - ∪  ∪| - ∪ ∪|-   - | -    ∪     ∪|- -
    sit tibi cura togae^potior pressumque quasillo
```

```
              - -   |  -    - |-||-∪∪ |-   ∪∪|-
             scortum quam Servi filia Sulpicia
```

```
     - ∪∪| -  - |  -   -| -    ∪ ∪ |- ∪ ∪| - -
     solliciti sunt pro nobis,^quibus illa dolori (e)st
```

```
            - - |    - -|- || - ∪   ∪ | -  ∪  ∪|-
            ne ced(am) ignoto maxima causa toro.
```

LIBER TERTIVS
(LYGDAMI ALIORVMQVE)
LYGDAMI ELEGIAE

1

Martis Romani festae uenere kalendae
(exoriens nostris hic fuit annus auis),
et uaga nunc certa discurrunt undique pompa
perque uias urbis munera perque domos.
dicite, Pierides, quonam donetur honore 5
seu mea, seu fallor, cara Neaera tamen.
' carmine formosae, pretio capiuntur auarae :
gaudeat, ut digna est, uersibus illa nouis.
lutea sed niueum inuoluat membrana libellum,
pumex et canas tondeat ante comas, 10
summaque praetexat tenuis fastigia chartae
indicet ut nomen littera facta tuum,
atque inter geminas pingantur cornua frontes :
sic etenim comptum mittere oportet opus.'
per uos, auctores huius mihi carminis, oro 15
Castaliamque umbram Pieriosque lacus,
ite domum cultumque illi donate libellum,
sicut erit : nullus defluat inde color.
illa mihi referet, si nostri mutua cura est,
an minor, an toto pectore deciderim. 20

Liber explicit secundus. Incipit tertius ad Neeram Amasiam suam
R^{ca} *A*
1 7-14 *cum Mureto Musis dedi*   7 precio capiuntur auari *Par.*
8 nouis *scripsi* : meis *A* : tuis *Muretus*   10 pumex et ψ : pumicet
et *A*   11 praetexat *g* : protexit *A*   carte *A*   12 picta *Liuineius*
tuum] meum ψ *uulg.*   15 per uos *g* : paruos *A*   16 umbram
g : umbrosam *A*   20 an maneam ψ

LYGDAMI ELEGIAE

sed primum meritam larga donate salute
atque haec submisso dicite uerba sono:
'haec tibi uir quondam, nunc frater, casta Neaera,
mittit et accipias munera parua rogat,
teque suis iurat caram magis esse medullis, 25
siue sibi coniunx siue futura soror:
sed potius coniunx: huius spem nominis illi
auferet extincto pallida Ditis aqua.'

II

Qvi primus caram iuueni carumque puellae
eripuit iuuenem, ferreus ille fuit.
durus et ille fuit, qui tantum ferre dolorem,
uiuere et erepta coniuge qui potuit.
non ego firmus in hoc, non haec patientia nostro 5
ingenio: frangit fortia corda dolor.
nec mihi uera loqui pudor est uitaeque fateri,
tot mala perpessae, taedia nata meae.
ergo cum tenuem fuero mutatus in umbram
candidaque ossa supra nigra fauilla teget, 10
ante meum ueniat longos incompta capillos
et fleat ante meum maesta Neaera rogum.
sed ueniat carae matris comitata dolore:
maereat haec genero, maereat illa uiro.
praefatae ante meos manes animamque recentem 15
perfusaeque pias ante liquore manus,
pars quae sola mei superabit corporis, ossa
incinctae nigra candida ueste legent,
et primum annoso spargent collecta lyaeo,
mox etiam niueo fundere lacte parent, 20

21 meritam *g*: meritum *A*   26 sibi *g*: tibi *A*
II 1, 2 habent *Fr*.   5 in *A* patien *tantum a prima manu*
tia ñro *ab altera erasis post* en III *uel* IV *litteris et nota quae super* en
steterat: patientia nostro *V*: patiemur et aequo *ψ*   6 frangit
fortia corda dolor *habent Par*.   7 est *g*: om. *A*   10 supra *A*:
super *g fort. recte*   15 recentem *scripsi*: rogate *A*: precatae *g*

post haec carbaseis umorem tollere uelis
   atque in marmorea ponere sicca domo.
illic quas mittit diues Panchaia merces
   Eoique Arabes, diues et Assyria,
et nostri memores lacrimae fundantur eodem: 25
   sic ego componi uersus in ossa uelim.
sed tristem mortis demonstret littera causam
   atque haec in celebri carmina fronte notet:
LYGDAMVS HIC SITVS EST: DOLOR HVIC ET CVRA NEAERAE,
   CONIVGIS EREPTAE, CAVSA PERIRE FVIT. 30

III

QVID prodest caelum uotis implesse, Neaera,
   blandaque cum multa tura dedisse prece,
non ut marmorei prodirem e limine tecti,
   insignis clara conspicuusque domo,
aut ut multa mei renouarent iugera tauri 5
   et magnas messes terra benigna daret,
sed tecum ut longae sociarem gaudia uitae
   inque tuo caderet nostra senecta sinu,
tunc cum permenso defunctus tempore lucis
   nudus Lethaea cogerer ire rate? 10
nam graue quid prodest pondus mihi diuitis auri,
   aruaque si findant pinguia mille boues?
quidue domus prodest Phrygiis innixa columnis,
   Taenare siue tuis, siue Caryste tuis,
et nemora in domibus sacros imitantia lucos 15
   aurataeque trabes marmoreumque solum?

21 uelis ψ: uentis A   23 illuc ψ fort. recte   23, 24 diues bis uix sanum: pinguis et A. ψ fort. recte   29 cura ψ: cã (=causa) A   Neaerae ψ: neera A
III 7 sociarem g: sociarent A   9 permensae ψ   11-13 habent Par.   11 Quid prodesse potest pondus graue d. a. Par.
14 cariste ψ: thariste A   16-22 habent Par.

LYGDAMI ELEGIAE

quidue in Erythraeo legitur quae litore concha
    tinctaque Sidonio murice lana iuuat,
et quae praeterea populus miratur? in illis
    inuidia est: falso plurima uulgus amat.   20
non opibus mentes hominum curaeque leuantur:
    nam Fortuna sua tempora lege regit.
sit mihi paupertas tecum iucunda, Neaera:
    at sine te regum munera nulla uolo.
o niueam quae te poterit mihi reddere lucem!   25
o mihi felicem terque quaterque diem!
at si, pro dulci reditu quaecumque uouentur,
    audiat auersa non meus aure deus,
nec me regna iuuant nec Lydius aurifer amnis
    nec quas terrarum sustinet orbis opes.   30
haec alii cupiant; liceat mihi paupere cultu
    securo cara coniuge posse frui.
adsis et timidis faueas, Saturnia, uotis,
    et faueas concha, Cypria, uecta tua.
aut si fata negant reditum tristesque sorores,   35
    stamina quae ducunt quaeque futura canunt,
me uocet in uastos amnes nigramque paludem
    diues in ignaua luridus Orcus aqua.

IV

Di meliora ferant, nec sint mihi somnia uera,
    quae tulit hesterna pessima nocte quies.

17 legitur qu(a)e *Par.* : legiturq; in *A*   20 inuidia est *Par.* :
inuida quae *A*   21, 22 *habent Fr.*   21 hominum *Fr. Par.* :
homini *A*   22 nam *A Par.* : nec *Fr.*   regit *Par.* : gerit *A Fr.*
24 at *g* : et *A*   28 auersa ψ : aduersa *A*   29-32 *habent*
Par.   29 non me *Par.*   lidius aurifer amnis *habent Fr.* : lidius
etiam *A Par.*   32 securo uitae munere p. f. *Par.*   35 tripli-
cesque *S. Allen coll. Ou. Met.* viii. 452 sq.   36 canunt *Heinsius* :
neunt *A soloece*   38 diues *merito suspectum*   luridus Orcus
habent Fr.

ite procul, uani, falsumque auertite uisum:
desinite in nobis quaerere uelle fidem.
diui uera monent, uenturae nuntia sortis
uera monent Tuscis exta probata uiris:
somnia fallaci ludunt temeraria nocte
et pauidas mentes falsa timere iubent?
et †natum maturas† hominum genus omina noctis
farre pio placant et saliente sale?
et tamen, utcumque est, siue illi uera moneri,
mendaci somno credere siue solent,
efficiat uanos noctis Lucina timores
et frustra immeritum pertimuisse uelit,
si mea nec turpi mens est obnoxia facto
nec laesit magnos impia lingua deos.
iam Nox aetherium nigris emensa quadrigis
mundum caeruleo lauerat amne rotas,
nec me sopierat menti deus utilis aegrae:
Somnus sollicitas deficit ante domos.
tandem, cum summo Phoebus prospexit ab ortu,
pressit languentis lumina sera quies.
hic iuuenis casta redimitus tempora lauro
est uisus nostra ponere sede pedem.
non illo quicquam formosius ulla priorum
aetas, humanum nec uidet ulla domus.
intonsi crines longa ceruice fluebant,
stillabat Syrio myrrhea rore coma.

IV 3, 4 *post* 16 *reponebam*: uanum ψ   nobis *Guyetus*: uotis *A*
7, 8 *habent Fr Par.*   9 natum in curas *uel* uanum metuens *uel* uatum
metuens ψ   11 monenti *g haud scio an recte*   12 solent *scripsi*:
uolent *A*   14 pertinuisse *A man. prima*   17 aetherium ψ:
ethereum *A*   emensa ψ: emersa *A*   19 sopierat *habent Fr.*
menti sopor utilis egre est *habent Par.*   21 summo... ab Oeta
Markland   26 humanum (*id est* hominum) *A*: heroum nec tulit
(*melius* dedit) *Lachmann*   ulla domus *Lachmann*: illud opus *A*
28 Syrio ψ: tyrio *A, cf.* vi. 63   myrrea *g*: mirthea *A*

LYGDAMI ELEGIAE

candor erat qualem praefert Latonia Luna,
   et color in niueo corpore purpureus,   30
ut iuueni primum uirgo deducta marito
   inficitur teneras ore rubente genas,
et cum contexunt amarantis alba puellae
   lilia et autumno candida mala rubent.
ima uidebatur talis inludere palla: 35
   namque haec in nitido corpore uestis erat.
artis opus rarae, fulgens testudine et auro
   pendebat laeua garrula parte lyra.
hanc primum ueniens plectro modulatus eburno
   felices cantus ore sonante dedit: 40
sed postquam fuerant digiti cum uoce locuti,
   edidit haec dulci tristia uerba modo:
'salue, cura deum: casto nam rite poetae
   Phoebusque et Bacchus Pieridesque fauent:
sed proles Semelae Bacchus doctaeque sorores   45
   dicere non norunt quid ferat hora sequens:
at mihi fatorum leges aeuique futuri
   euentura pater posse uidere dedit.
quare ego quae dico non fallax accipe uates
   quamque deus uero Cynthius ore ferar.   50
tantum cara tibi quantum nec filia matri,
   quantum nec cupido bella puella uiro,
pro qua sollicitas caelestia numina uotis,
   quae tibi securos non sinit ire dies
et, cum te fusco Somnus uelauit amictu,   55
   uanum nocturnis fallit imaginibus,
carminibus celebrata tuis formosa Neaera
⁌ alterius mauult esse puella uiri,

33 aut cum *ψ*   41 loquti *A*   42 dulci tristia *Broukhusius*: tristi dulcia *A*   45 semele *A*   47 euique *A*: cuique *V*   50 quamque *scripsi Classical Quarterly* t. vi, p. 40: quidque *A*: quodque *g uulg.*   ferar *scripsi*: ferat *A*: feram *Broukhusius uulg.*

[TIBVLLI LIB. III. IV]

diuersasque suas agitat mens impia curas,
nec gaudet casta nupta Neaera domo. 60
a crudele genus nec fidum femina nomen!
a pereat, didicit fallere si qua uirum.
sed flecti poterit : mens est mutabilis illis:
tu modo cum multa bracchia tende prece.
saeuus Amor docuit ualidos temptare labores, 65
saeuus Amor docuit uerbera posse pati.
me quondam Admeti niueas pauisse iuuencas
non est in uanum fabula ficta iocum:
tunc ego nec cithara poteram gaudere sonora
nec similes chordis reddere uoce sonos, 70
sed perlucenti cantum meditabar auena
ille ego Latonae filius atque Iouis.
nescis quid sit amor, iuuenis, si ferre recusas
immitem dominam coniugiumque ferum.
ergo ne dubita blandas adhibere querellas: 75
uincuntur molli pectora dura prece.
quod si uera canunt sacris oracula templis,
haec illi nostro nomine dicta refer:
hoc tibi coniugium promittit Delius ipse;
felix hoc alium desine uelle uirum.' 80
dixit, et ignauus defluxit corpore somnus.
a ego ne possim tanta uidere mala.
nec tibi crediderim uotis contraria uota
nec tantum crimen pectore inesse tuo.

59 suis *Muretus*: tuis *Lipsius*   60 neaera *g*: nerea *A*
63 mens est mutabilis illis *habent Par.*   64 prece ψ: fide *A*
65 *habuit F* (*uetus fragmentum Cuiacii quod hic uidetur incepisse*) : *om.
A* : saeuus amor docuit dominae fera uerba minantis *Cuiacianus*
ualidos] uarios *L. Mueller*   labores] leones *Huschke*   66 habent
Fr.   posse *A Fr.* : saeua *F*   69 canora ψ   71 cantus
Plant(*iniana editio*) *fort. F*: cantu *in* cantus *mutatum Cuiacianus*
76 habent *Par.*   80 hoc *F teste Scaligero in castigationibus et
Plant. in contextu*: ac *A Cuiacianus cuius lectionem Scaliger in marg.
Plant. adscripsit*   81 corpore *A Cuiacianus Plant.*: pectore ψ

LYGDAMI ELEGIAE

nam te nec uasti genuerunt aequora ponti 85
  nec flammam uoluens ore Chimaera fero
nec canis anguina redimitus terga caterua,
  cui tres sunt linguae tergeminumque caput,
Scyllaque uirgineam canibus succincta figuram,
  nec te conceptam saeua leaena tulit, 90
barbara nec Scythiae tellus horrendaue Syrtis;
  sed culta et duris non habitanda domus
et longe ante alias omnes mitissima mater
  isque pater quo non alter amabilior.
haec deus in melius crudelia somnia uertat 95
  et iubeat tepidos inrita ferre Notos.

V

Vos tenet, Etruscis manat quae fontibus unda,
  unda sub aestiuum non adeunda Canem,
nunc autem sacris Baiarum proxima lymphis,
  cum se purpureo uere remittit humus.
at mihi Persephone nigram denuntiat horam: 5
  immerito iuueni parce nocere, dea.
non ego temptaui nulli temeranda uirorum
  audax laudandae sacra docere deae,
nec mea mortiferis infecit pocula sucis
  dextera nec cuiquam trita uenena dedit, 10
nec nos sacrilegos templis admouimus ignes,
  nec cor sollicitant facta nefanda meum,

---

87 canis anguina *scripsi*: canis anguinea *g Cuiacianus Plant.*: consanguinea *A*   89 succincta *F*: submixta *A Cuiacianus*   92 diris *Plant.*   96 irrita ψ *Plant.*: impia *A Cuiacianus*
V 1 Vos *g Plant.*: Os *V*: Nos *A*   3 proxima *Scioppius*: maxima *A Plant.*   7 uirorum ψ: deor uirorum *Cuiacianus* (cf. *Scaligerum in castigg.*): deorum *A Plant.* (et, ut suspicor, *F*): piorum ψ   8 celandae ψ   10 trita *F teste Scaligero in castigg.*: certa *A Plant. Cuiacianus*   11 sacrilegos *g Plant.*: sacrilegis *A*: sacrilegi *Cuiacianus cetera ut A*   admouimus *g Plant.*: amouimus *A*   ignes *g Plant.*: egros *A*   12 *Par.* habent sollicitant pectus facta nefanda reum   facta] furta *Baehrens*

nec nos insanae meditantes iurgia mentis
impia in aduersos soluimus ora deos.
et nondum cani nigros laesere capillos, 15
nec uenit tardo curua senecta pede.
natalem primo nostrum uidere parentes,
cum cecidit fato consul uterque pari.
quid fraudare iuuat uitem crescentibus uuis
et modo nata mala uellere poma manu? 20
parcite, pallentes undas quicumque tenetis
duraque sortiti tertia regna dei.
Elysios olim liceat cognoscere campos
Lethaeamque ratem Cimmeriosque lacus,
cum mea rugosa pallebunt ora senecta 25
et referam pueris tempora prisca senex.
atque utinam uano nequiquam terrear aestu!
languent ter quinos sed mea membra dies.
at uobis Tuscae celebrantur numina lymphae
et facilis lenta pellitur unda manu. 30
uiuite felices, memores et uiuite nostri,
siue erimus seu nos fata fuisse uelint.
interea nigras pecudes promittite Diti
et niuei lactis pocula mixta mero.

VI

CANDIDE Liber ades: sic sit tibi mystica uitis
semper, sic hedera tempora uincta feras:
aufer et ipse meum patera medicante dolorem:
saepe tuo cecidit munere uictus Amor.

13 meditantes *g Plant*. : meditantis *A*   15, 16 *habent Par.*
15 sepe quidem cani *Par*.   16 nec uenit tacito *Par*.   19,
20 *habent Fr. Par*.   27 nequicquam ψ : necquicquam *A*   29
at uobis *g* : at nobis *Cuiacianus* : atq; nobis *A*   32 uolent ψ
VI 1 uitis *g* : uictis *A*   2 edera *habent Fr*.   geras *g Statius
fort. recte*   3 patera medicante *Waardenburg* : pariter medicando
A Plant. : pariles medicate *ipse temptaui*

LYGDAMI ELEGIAE

care puer, madeant generoso pocula baccho,　　　5
　et nobis prona funde Falerna manu.
ite procul durum curae genus, ite labores:
　fulserit hic niueis Delius alitibus.
uos modo proposito dulces faueatis amici,
　neue neget quisquam me duce se comitem :　　10
aut si quis uini certamen mite recusat,
　fallat eum tecto cara puella dolo.
ille facit mites animos deus, ille ferocem
　contudit et dominae misit in arbitrium;
Armenias tigres et fuluas ille leaenas　　15
　uicit et indomitis mollia corda dedit.
haec Amor et maiora ualet. sed poscite Bacchi
　munera : quem uestrum pocula sicca iuuant?
conuenit ex aequo nec toruus Liber in illis
　qui se quique una uina iocosa colunt :　　20
†non uenit iratus nimium nimiumque seuerus† :
　qui timet irati numina magna, bibat.
quales his poenas qualis quantusque minetur,
　Cadmeae matris praeda cruenta docet.
sed procul a nobis hic sit timor, illaque, si qua est,　　25
　quid ualeat laesi sentiat ira dei.
quid precor a demens? uenti temeraria uota,
　aeriae et nubes diripienda ferant.
quamuis nulla mei superest tibi cura, Neaera,
　sis felix et sint candida fata tua.　　30.

6 et *A Plant.* : i ψ　　7 *habent Par.*　　cure durum *Par.*
8 fulserit *g Cuiacianus Plant.* : pulserit *A*　　Delius] Idalis *temptaui*,
Housman antea Idaliis hic Venus *al.*　　13 *habent Par.*　　mites ψ :
dites *A*　　feroces *g Par.*　　15 Armenias *g* : Armenas *A*　　16
habent Par.　　17 ualet ψ : uolet *A Plant.*　　20 uina] uerba *Bolle*
21 conuenit ... seueros *Lachmann* : iam uenit ψ *Plant.*　　*fort.* nam
uenit ... seueris (*hoc Liuineius*)　　23 qualis *F* : deus hic *A*
quantūq; *A*　　25, 26 iraque si qua est ... illa dei *Huschke*

[TIBVLLI LIB. III. VI]

at nos securae reddamus tempora mensae:
uenit post multas una serena dies.
ei mihi, difficile est imitari gaudia falsa,
difficile est tristi fingere mente iocum,
nec bene mendaci risus componitur ore, 35
nec bene sollicitis ebria uerba sonant.
quid queror infelix? turpes discedite curae:
odit Lenaeus tristia uerba pater.
Gnosia, Theseae quondam periuria linguae
fleuisti ignoto sola relicta mari: 40
sic cecinit pro te doctus, Minoi, Catullus
ingrati referens impia facta uiri.
uos ego nunc moneo: felix, quicumque dolore
alterius disces posse cauere tuom.
nec uos aut capiant pendentia bracchia collo 45
aut fallat blanda sordida lingua prece.
etsi perque suos fallax iurauit ocellos
Iunonemque suam perque suam Venerem,
nulla fides inerit: periuria ridet amantum
Iuppiter et uentos inrita ferre iubet. 50
ergo quid totiens fallacis uerba puellae
conqueror? ite a me, seria uerba, precor.
quam uellem tecum longas requiescere noctes
et tecum longos peruigilare dies,
perfida nec merito nobis †inimica merenti† 55
perfida, sed, quamuis perfida, cara tamen!

32 multas *A Plant.*: multos *Cuiacianus*   33 *nouum carmen incipit in A*: *cum priore iunxit Muretus*   33-36 *habent Fr. Par.*
33 ei] hei ψ: et *Fr.*: si *A*: i *V*: heu quam d. *Par.*   34 locum *Fr. man. prima*   35, 36 nec] non *bis Par.*   43, 44 felix ... tuom *habent Fr. Par.*   44 disces *A Fr. Plant.*: didicit *Par.*
cauere *Fr. Par. F*: carere *A*   tuom *Baehrens*: tuos *F*: tuo *A Fr.*: suum *Par.*   45, 46 *habent Par.*   45 ne uos decipiant *Par.*
46 nec capiat blanda *Par.*   sordida *A Par. Plant.*: subdola *Heinsius*   prece *Par. g*: fide *A Plant.*   47 iurabit ψ   51 quid ψ *Plant.*: qui *A Cuiacianus*   52 *habent Fr.*   procul ψ

LYGDAMI ELEGIAE

Naida Bacchus amat: cessas, o lente minister?
   temperet annosum Marcia lympha merum.
non ego, si fugit nostrae conuiuia mensae
   ignotum cupiens uana puella torum,   60
sollicitus repetam tota suspiria nocte.
   tu, puer, i, liquidum fortius adde merum.
iam dudum Syrio madefactus tempora nardo
   debueram sertis implicuisse comas.

DE SVLPICIA

INCERTI AVCTORIS ELEGIAE

[TIBVLLI LIB. III. VIII = IV. II]

SVLPICIA est tibi culta tuis, Mars magne, kalendis:
   spectatum e caelo, si sapis, ipse ueni.
hoc Venus ignoscet: at tu, uiolente, caueto
   ne tibi miranti turpiter arma cadant.

   196 pronum *Burmann*   197 quodcumque ψ *Plant.*: quidcunque *A*   198 sit m.] sin m. *F*   200 nec *g Plant.*: *om. A* uincere *F*: mittere *A*   202 *alterum* uel *om. F ut uidetur*: habet *Cuiacianus*   203 statuent *g Plant.*: statuunt *A*   205 celerem *F*: fato *A*   206 figura *A Cuiacianus*: figuram *Plant.*   210 quandocunque *F*: inquēcunq; *A*
   VIII Laus Sulpitie ad deum martem R^{ca} *A*   3 tu uiolente caueto habent *Fr.*   4 habent *Fr.*

[TIBVLLI LIB. III. VIII]

illius ex oculis, cum uult exurere diuos,　　　　5
  accendit geminas lampadas acer Amor.
illam, quidquid agit, quoquo uestigia mouit,
  componit furtim subsequiturque Decor.
seu soluit crines, fusis decet esse capillis :
  seu compsit, comptis est ueneranda comis.　　10
urit, seu Tyria uoluit procedere palla :
  urit, seu niuea candida ueste uenit.
talis in aeterno felix Vertumnus Olympo
  mille habet ornatus, mille decenter habet.
sola puellarum digna est cui mollia caris　　　15
  uellera det sucis bis madefacta Tyros,
possideatque, metit quidquid bene olentibus aruis
  cultor odoratae diues Arabs segetis,
et quascumque niger Rubro de litore gemmas
  proximus Eois colligit Indus aquis.　　　　20
hanc uos, Pierides, festis cantate kalendis,
  et testudinea Phoebe superbe lyra.
hoc sollemne sacrum multos haec sumet in annos :
  dignior est uestro nulla puella choro.

[TIBVLLI LIB. III. IX = IV. III]

PARCE meo iuueni, seu quis bona pascua campi
  seu colis umbrosi deuia montis aper,
nec tibi sit duros acuisse in proelia dentes ;
  incolumem custos hunc mihi seruet Amor.

  .　　.　　.　　.　　.　　.　　.

sed procul abducit uenandi Delia cura :　　　　5
  o pereant siluae deficiantque canes !

13 uertūnus *habent Fr.*　　14 habet *g Plant. Cuiacianus qui*
ht : hūc *A*　　23 haec sumet *F* : hoc sumet *A Cuiacianus*　　24
choro *g Plant. Cuiacianus* : thoro *A*
  IX 3 praelia *F* : pectore *A*　　*post* 4 *uersus duo uel plures excidisse uidentur*

DE SVLPICIA

quis furor est, quae mens densos indagine colles
   claudentem teneras laedere uelle manus?
quidue iuuat furtim latebras intrare ferarum
   candidaque hamatis crura notare rubis?   10
sed tamen, ut tecum liceat, Cerinthe, uagari,
   ipsa ego per montes retia torta feram,
ipsa ego uelocis quaeram uestigia cerui
   et demam celeri ferrea uincla cani.
tunc mihi, tunc placeant siluae, si, lux mea, tecum   15
   arguar ante ipsas concubuisse plagas:
tunc ueniat licet ad casses, inlaesus abibit,
   ne ueneris cupidae gaudia turbet, aper.
nunc sine me sit nulla uenus, sed lege Dianae,
   caste puer, casta retia tange manu: 20
et quaecumque meo furtim subrepit amori,
   incidat in saeuas diripienda feras.
at tu uenandi studium concede parenti,
   et celer in nostros ipse recurre sinus.

[TIBVLLI LIB. III. X = IV. IV]

Hvc ades et tenerae morbos expelle puellae,
   huc ades, intonsa Phoebe superbe coma.
crede mihi, propera: nec te iam, Phoebe, pigebit
   formosae medicas applicuisse manus.
effice ne macies pallentes occupet artus,   5
   neu notet informis candida membra color,
et quodcumque mali est et quidquid triste timemus,
   in pelagus rapidis euehat amnis aquis.
sancte, ueni, tecumque feras, quicumque sapores,
   quicumque et cantus corpora fessa leuant: 10
neu iuuenem torque, metuit qui fata puellae
   uotaque pro domina uix numeranda facit.

---

10 hāmatis *habent Fr.*   18 ne *g Plant. Cuiacianus*: da *A*
19 nunc ψ: tunc *A Plant.*   20 tange *AF*   21 et *A*: at *F*
surrepet *Cuiacianus*
X 6 candida ψ: pallida *A*   8 rapidis *V*: rabidis *A*

[TIBVLLI LIB. III. X]

interdum uouet, interdum, quod langueat illa,
  dicit in aeternos aspera uerba deos.
pone metum, Cerinthe; deus non laedit amantes.   15
  tu modo semper ama: salua puella tibi est.
nil opus est fletu: lacrimis erit aptius uti,   21
  si quando fuerit tristior illa tibi.   22
at nunc tota tua est, te solum candida secum   17
  cogitat, et frustra credula turba sedet.
Phoebe, faue: laus magna tibi tribuetur in uno
  corpore seruato restituisse duos.   20
iam celeber, iam laetus eris, cum debita reddet   23
  certatim sanctis laetus uterque focis.
tunc te felicem dicet pia turba deorum,   25
  optabunt artes et sibi quisque tuas.

[TIBVLLI LIB. III. XI = IV. V]

Qvi mihi te, Cerinthe, dies dedit, hic mihi sanctus
  atque inter festos semper habendus erit.
te nascente nouum Parcae cecinere puellis
  seruitium et dederunt regna superba tibi.
uror ego ante alias: iuuat hoc, Cerinthe, quod uror,   5
  si tibi de nobis mutuus ignis adest.
mutuus adsit amor, per te dulcissima furta
  perque tuos oculos per Geniumque rogo.
magne Geni, cape tura libens uotisque faueto,
  si modo, cum de me cogitat, ille calet.   10
quod si forte alios iam nunc suspirat amores,
  tum precor infidos, sancte, relinque focos.

21, 22 *post* 16 *reposuit* ψ   17 at *V*: ac *A*   24 laetus] gratus *Martinon*: lotus *Broukhusius* (lautus *Haupt* in u. 23)
  XI 1 Qui mihi *F*: Est qui *A*: St qui *V*   4 dederunt *g Plant.* : dederant *A Cuiacianus*   6 ne ψ: ne de *A*   7 per te *AF*   9 magne ψ: mane *A Plant.*   10 calet ψ: ualet *A*: uolet *F*   11 suspirat ψ *Plant.*: suspiret *A*   12 tum ψ: tunc *A*

DE SVLPICIA

nec tu sis iniusta, Venus : uel seruiat aeque
uinctus uterque tibi uel mea uincla leua.
sed potius ualida teneamur uterque catena,   15
nulla queat posthac quam soluisse dies.
optat idem iuuenis quod nos, sed tectius optat :
nam pudet haec illum dicere uerba palam.
at tu, Natalis, quoniam deus omnia sentis,
adnue : quid refert, clamne palamne roget ?   20

[TIBVLLI LIB. III. XII = IV. VI]

NATALIS Iuno, sanctos cape turis aceruos,
quos tibi dat tenera docta puella manu.
tota tibi est hodie, tibi se laetissima compsit,
staret ut ante tuos conspicienda focos.
illa quidem ornandi causas tibi, diua, relegat :   5
est tamen, occulte cui placuisse uelit.
at tu, sancta, faue, neu quis diuellat amantes,
sed iuueni quaeso mutua uincla para.
sic bene compones : ullae non ille puellae
seruire aut cuiquam dignior illa uiro.   10
nec possit cupidos uigilans deprendere custos
fallendique uias mille ministret Amor.
adnue purpureaque ueni perlucida palla :
ter tibi fit libo, ter, dea casta, mero,
praecipit et natae mater studiosa quod optet :   15
illa aliud tacita iam sua mente rogat.
uritur ut celeres urunt altaria flammae,
nec, liceat quamuis, sana fuisse uelit.

16 quam ψ : hanc *Rossberg Palmer* : om. *A in* III *litterarum spatio*
17 tectius ψ : tutius *A Plant.*   18 haec *g Plant. Cuiacianus* : hic *A·*
20 referet *V* : referet *A*   clamne palamne ψ *Plant.* : clamue palamue *A*
   XII 3 tota] lota *Guyetus*   5 ornandi *g Plant.* : orandi *A*
7 neu quis *F* : ne nos *A*   9 ullae *AF*   10 cuiquam *g Plant. Cuiacianus* : cuidam *A*   13 -que *g Plant. Cuiacianus* :. om. *A*   14 fit *g* : sic *A Cuiacianus* : sit *Plant.*   mero, (*add.* mero.) *interpunxi*   15 optat *A*   16 sua *AF* : tua *Baehrens*

[TIBVLLI LIB. III. XII]

†sis iuueni grata, ueniet cum proximus annus†,
hic idem uotis iam uetus adsit amor.   20

SVLPICIAE ELEGIDIA

[TIBVLLI LIB. III. XIII = IV. VII]

TANDEM uenit amor, qualem texisse pudori
quam nudasse alicui sit mihi fama magis.
exorata meis illum Cytherea Camenis
attulit in nostrum deposuitque sinum.
exoluit promissa Venus: mea gaudia narret,   5
dicetur si quis non habuisse sua.
non ego signatis quicquam mandare tabellis,
me legat ut nemo quam meus ante, uelim,
sed peccasse iuuat, uultus componere famae
taedet: cum digno digna fuisse ferar.   10

[TIBVLLI LIB. III. XIV = IV. VIII]

INVISVS natalis adest, qui rure molesto
et sine Cerintho tristis agendus erit.
dulcius urbe quid est? an uilla sit apta puellae
atque Arretino frigidus amnis agro?

19 sis *F* : si *A* : sic *Statius*   grata] *fort.* grate : gratum *Statius* : sis, luno, grata ac *Gruppe* : grata ut *Eberz*   ueniet *A Cuiacianus* : adueniet *Plant.*   20 iam ratus *Prien*   adsit ψ : esset *A*
XIII Gratulatio ad uenerem de amoris obtentu R^ca *A*
 1 *bis scriptus in A cum titulum carminis et praecedat et sequatur*   pudori *A priore loco* : pudore *posteriore*   2 minor ψ
6 sua *F* : suam *A*   8 me *A* : ne *g Plant.*   ut *Cuiacianus* : id *A Plant.*   nemo *g Plant. Cuiacianus* : uenio *A*   quam ψ, qm *A*
XIV *Titulus in* A Messale R^ca, *in F* Sulpitia ad Messallam *cf. Hiller Rheinisches Museum a* 1874 *p.* 106
 4 Arretino *g Cuiacianus* : aretino *A Plant.* : Reatino *Huschke* Arnus ψ

SVLPICIAE ELEGIDIA

iam, nimium Messalla mei studiose, quiescas; 5
non tempestiuae saepe, propinque, uiae.
hic animum sensusque meos abducta relinquo,
arbitrio quam uis non sinit esse meo.

[TIBVLLI LIB. III. XV = IV. IX]

Scis iter ex animo sublatum triste puellae?
natali Romae iam licet esse tuo.
omnibus ille dies nobis natalis agatur,
qui nec opinanti nunc tibi forte uenit.

[TIBVLLI LIB. III. XVI = IV. X]

Gratvm est, securus multum quod iam tibi de me
permittis, subito ne male inepta cadam.
sit tibi cura togae potior pressumque quasillo
scortum quam Serui filia Sulpicia:
solliciti sunt pro nobis, quibus illa dolori est 5
ne cedam ignoto maxima causa toro.

[TIBVLLI LIB. III. XVII = IV. XI]

Estne tibi, Cerinthe, tuae pia cura puellae,
quod mea nunc uexat corpora fessa calor?
a ego non aliter tristes euincere morbos
optarim, quam te si quoque uelle putem.
at mihi quid prosit morbos euincere, si tu 5
nostra potes lento pectore ferre mala?

    6 non ψ *Cuiacianus Plant.*: neu *A*   uiae *plurale esse primus intellexit Némethy*   8 quam uis *Statius*: quamuis *A Plant.*   sinit *Statius*: sinis *A*
    XV 2 iam licet *F*: non sinet *A*   tuo *AF uix recte*: suo ψ: meo *Huschke*   3, 4 *grauiter corrupti*   o. i. bonis diues n. a. | q. n. opinata n. t. forte (*uel* sorte) u. *Housman*: forte o. i. d. annis tam laetus (tam l. *Baehrens*) a. | quam (*hoc Baehrens*) etc.
    XVI 1 tibi ψ: mihi *A*   2 promittis *Heinsius*   5 doloris *Rigler, cum* causa *coniungendum*   6 nec *A Cuiacianus Plant.* cedam *Statius*: credam *A Cuiacianus Plant.*   causa *AF*
    XVII 1 pia cura ψ: placitura *A*   3 a] ha *A*: ah *V*: ha *in* ah *mutatum Cuiacianus*   5 at *F*: ah *V*: ha *A*   si *g V corr.*: quid *AV Cuiacianus Plant.*   6 lento *F Cui.*: leto *A Cui. marg.*

[TIBVLLI LIB. III. XVIII = IV. XII]

NE tibi sim, mea lux, aeque iam feruida cura
   ac uideor paucos ante fuisse dies,
si quicquam tota commisi stulta iuuenta
   cuius me fatear paenituisse magis,
hesterna quam te solum quod nocte reliqui,   5
   ardorem cupiens dissimulare meum.

INCERTI AVCTORIS CARMINA

[TIBVLLI LIB. III. XIX = IV. XIII]

NVLLA tuum nobis subducet femina lectum:
   hoc primum iuncta est foedere nostra uenus.
tu mihi sola places, nec iam te praeter in urbe
   formosa est oculis ulla puella meis.
atque utinam posses uni mihi bella uideri!   5
   displiceas aliis: sic ego tutus ero.
nil opus inuidia est, procul absit gloria uulgi:
   qui sapit, in tacito gaudeat ille sinu.
sic ego secretis possum bene uiuere siluis,
   qua nulla humano sit uia trita pede.   10
tu mihi curarum requies, tu nocte uel atra
   lumen, et in solis tu mihi turba locis.
nunc licet e caelo mittatur amica Tibullo,
   mittetur frustra deficietque uenus.
hoc tibi sancta tuae Iunonis numina iuro,   15
   quae sola ante alios est mihi magna deos.

XVIII *Adhaeret priori in A in quo bis exstat cum hic tum post Lygdami el.* vi
  1 ne *A priore loco, hic* nec   sim *A hic,* sit *priore loco*   iam *A hic,* tam *priore loco*   2 ac *AF*   uideor *FA priore loco,* uideas *A hic*
  XIX *Alloquitur puellam et amasiam innominatam A*
  3 mihi ψ *Plant.* : mõ (= modo) *A*   5 possis ψ   8 ille ψ *Plant.* : ipse *A*   15 hec *V*: haec per *Plant.*   16 mihi 'libri nostri' *h. e. F Scaliger in cast.* : tibi *A Cuiacianus Plant.*

[TIBVLLI]

quid facio demens? heu heu mea pignora cedo.
   iuraui stulte : proderat iste timor.
nunc tu fortis eris, nunc tu me audacius ures :
   hoc peperit misero garrula lingua malum.   20
iam faciam quodcumque uoles, tuus usque manebo,
   nec fugiam notae seruitium dominae,
sed Veneris sanctae considam uinctus ad aras :
   haec notat iniustos supplicibusque fauet.

[TIBVLLI LIB. III. XX = IV. XIV]

Rvmor ait crebro nostram peccare puellam :
   nunc ego me surdis auribus esse uelim.
crimina non haec sunt nostro sine facta dolore :
   quid miserum torques, rumor acerbe ? tace.

THE MINOR AUTHORS OF THE CORPUS TIBULLIANUM

LYGDAMUS 1
([Tib.] 3.1)

Dedication: A present for Neaera on the day of the Matronalia.

1. **Martis...kalendae:** 1st March, the day of the *Matronalia* or the so-called "women's kalends" when presents were given to women.
   Romani: Mars was, after Jupiter, the chief Roman god, and according to legend was the father of the city's founder, Romulus.
   uenere = *uenerunt.*
2. **exoriens** < *exorior,* "rise, appear above the horizon." Lit.: "This was the rising year," trans.: "the year's beginning." Until 153 BC the Roman calendar consisted of only ten months, March to December. March 1st was, therefore, the old "New Year's Day."
3. **uaga:** with *munera* (4). The same idea is present in *discurrunt.* Trans.: "presents are travelling in different directions."
   certa...pompa: "in sure procession," i.e. destined for their individual recipients.
   undique: "from every direction."
5. **Pierides:** A name for the Muses, derived from Pieria, a district in SE Macedonia connected with their worship.
   donetur < *donare* + accusative of person to whom gift is given + ablative of gift (cf. English "endow" [somebody with something]); subjunctive in indirect question.
6. **seu mea...tamen:** "Neaera, dear if she be mine, and dear still even if I am mistaken."
7. **formosae:** sc. *puellae.*
   pretio: "by money."
   capiuntur: "are won over."
8. **gaudeat:** jussive.
   ut digna est: i.e., "as becomes her" (being *formosa,* not *avara).*
9. **inuoluat** < *inuoluo,* "cover, envelop."
   membrana: a covering of parchment.

libellum: "scroll." The diminutive of *liber* is used because Lygdamus' poetry is elegy, not a "major" genre of poetry (like epic or tragedy).
10. pumex: A piece of pumice was used to polish scrolls to remove fragments of papyrus (here referred to metaphorically as *canas...comas*).
   ante: adverbial: "first."
11. summa...fastigia: "the very top" (object of *praetexat*).
   praetexat: jussive, "border" or "edge." The subject is *littera facta* (12).
12. indicet ut: result clause with *littera facta* again as subject.
13. geminas...frontes: the two ends of the papyrus roll.
   cornua: the knobs or bosses affixed to the ends of the two sticks around which the papyrus was wound.
14. sic...comptum: "dressed like that." *comptum* < *como*.
   oportet: sc. *te*.
15 per: as often in prayers, separated from the nouns which it governs, *Castaliamque umbram Pieriosque lacus*.
   uos: object of *oro*.
   mihi: dative of advantage.
16. Castaliam < *Castalius*, "pertaining to Castalia," a fountain on Mt. Parnassus, near Delphi, associated with Apollo, god of music and poetry, and with the Muses.
   Pieriosque lacus: See on 5. *lacus* refers to the springs of Pieria.
17. donate: here with direct and indirect object (like *dare*).
18. inde: "from it."
   color: "freshness."
19. referet < *refero*, "reply."
   nostri: objective genitive, "of me." As often in poetry, a "royal plural."
   cura: "love," as often in elegy.
20. minor: sc. *cura*.
   deciderim: future perfect, < *decido*, "fall, drop from."
21. meritam: sc. *eam*: "as she deserves." Direct object of *donate* (see on 5).
   salute: "greeting." *Salus* is the word conventionally used at the beginning of a letter.
22. submisso...sono: ablative of manner; "in hushed tones."
23. uir: usually used in elegy of a husband, as here, but sometimes of a lover.
   frater: "lover." See OLD s.v. *frater* 3b.
24. accipias: "paratactic" subjunctive, or indirect command, dependent on *rogat*: "asks you to accept" (Woodcock §134).

25. **suis...medullis:** ablative of comparison: "than his own heart" (lit. "marrow").
26. **siue sibi coniunx:** sc. *eris*.
   coniunx: usually, but not necessarily, a husband or wife in elegy. Here (in view of line 23) it probably means "wife."
   soror: cf. *frater* (23). OLD s.v. *soror* 1d.
27. **sed potius coniunx:** sc. *sis*.
   potius: "rather, preferably."
   nominis: "title" (i.e., of *coniunx*).
   illi: "from him" (i.e., Lygdamus). Dative of disadvantage after a verb of depriving (*auferet* [28]). (Woodcock §61).
28. **extincto** < *exstinguo*; dative, agreeing with *illi* (27).
   pallida: conventional epithet of the Underworld, because pallor is associated with death.
   Ditis: "of Dis" (Roman ruler of the Underworld).

LYGDAMUS 2 ([Tib.] 3.2)

Loss of Neaera turns Lygdamus' thoughts towards his own death and funeral.

1. **qui:** Supply *ille* (2) as antecedent: "That man who......".
   caram: sc. *puellam*.
   iuueni...puellae: datives of disadvantage after a verb of depriving, *eripere*. See on Lygdamus 1.27.
2. **ferreus:** "iron-hearted, cruel."
3. **ferre:** governed (as also *uiuere* [4]) by *potuit* (4).
4. **coniuge:** See on *Lygdamus* 1.26.
5. **non ego:** sc. *sum*.
   in hoc: "in this respect."
5-6. **non haec patientia** (sc. *est*) **nostro ingenio:** "my character does not have this fortitude." *nostro ingenio* is possessive dative.
7. **mihi...pudor est** + infinitive: "I feel ashamed [to]."
7-8. **fateri:** governs indirect statement: *tot mala...taedia nata (esse)*.
8. **taedia:** "weariness, aversion (to)" + genitive.
   perpessae (sc. *vitae*) < *perpetior*, "suffer, endure."
9. **fuero mutatus:** = *ero mutatus*.
   umbram: "shade, ghost."
10. **supra:** adverbial.
11. **ante meum:** sc. *rogum* (12).
   ueniat: The subject, Neaera, is to be supplied from line 12.
   longos...capillos: "internal" accusative with passive participle *incompta* (Woodcock §19 [ii]). Lit.: "dishevelled as to her long hair." Trans.: "with her long hair dishevelled."

13. **comitata** + ablative: "accompanied (by)."
   dolore: abstract for concrete. Lit.: "by the grief of her beloved mother," i.e. by her grieving mother.
14. **haec...illa:** "the latter...the former."
15. **praefatae** < *praefor*. "address a preliminary prayer to." *ante*, adverbial, is thus almost redundant. The subject "they" is Neaera and her mother.
   manes: "shade of the dead," always in the plural.
   recentem: "freshly departed."
16. **pias...manus:** "internal" accusative (see on line 11) after *perfusae* (< *perfundo*, "wet, drench"). Translate: "first wetting their dutiful hands."
17. **pars quae...corporis:** in apposition to *ossa*, which follows. *pars* is "attracted" into the nominative by *quae*, which is the subject of *superabit*.
18. **incinctae** < *incinctus* + ablative: "dressed in." *nigra* goes with *ueste*, and *candida* with *ossa* (17).
19. **collecta:** i.e., the bones.
   lyaeo: "wine" (from Lyaeus, a cult-title of Dionysus, god of wine).
20. **fundere:** "to drench (with)."
   parent < *paro*, "prepare" (to carry out an action). Note the switch to jussive subjunctive from the future (*legent* [18], *spargent* [19]).
21. **carbaseis...velis:** instrumental ablative: "with cloths of linen."
   tollere: "to remove," governed by *parent* (20).
22. **ponere:** sc. *parent*.
   sicca: "when dry."
   domo: i.e., the tomb, the "home" of the dead person.
23. **illic:** either "there" (in the tomb) or "then, next." The verb *fundantur* must be supplied from 25.
   quas: *merces* ("commodities, merchandise") is antecedent. The reference is to incense.
   Panchaia: an imaginary island in the Indian Ocean, here used as representative of the distant East.
24. **Eoi** < *Eous, -a, -um*, "eastern." The Arabs, and the East in general, symbolised riches and luxurious living for the Romans.
   et: postponed.
25. **nostri:** objective genitive with *memores*, "mindful, remembering." For the plural, see on *Lygdamus* 1.19.
   fundantur: jussive subjunctive, with *merces* and *lacrimae* as subjects.
   eodem: "in the same place," i.e., the tomb.
26. **componi:** "to be buried."
   uersus in ossa: "when turned to bones."
   uelim: potential: "I would like."

27. **demonstret:** jussive.
littera: here "an inscription" (OLD 6.b).
28. **in celebri...fronte:** lit.: "on its famous face," i.e., on the face (of the gravestone) which will become famous because it is dedicated to Lygdamus.
carmina: here "verses."
29. **hic situs est:** "here is buried," a conventional epitaphic formula.
huic: dative of disadvantage.
dolor...et cura Neaerae: Take *dolor* and *cura* as a hendiadys (i.e. one idea formulated in two words or expressions): "his heart-rending love for Neaera."
huic: dative of disadvantage.
30. **coniugis ereptae:** in apposition to *Neaerae*.
causa perire fuit: "was cause (for him) to die," i.e., caused his death.

LYGDAMUS 3 ([Tib.] 3.3)

Without Neaera Wealth is Nothing

1. **Quid prodest + infinitive:** a common formula. *prodesse* = "to be of advantage, profit." So, here, "What is the use [of]...?"
uotis: i.e., Lygdamus' vows. A *uotum* is a prayer made to a god, with an accompanying promise of an offering if the prayer is granted. On the granting, the individual is under obligation (*uoti reus*) to fulfil the promise (*uotum reddere*).
implesse: syncopated form of *implevisse*, < *implere*.
2. **blanda...tura:** "propitiatory frankincense." *tus* (frankincense) was often used as a religious offering. *blandus*, literally "persuasive," refers to its efficacy.
3-6. What Lygdamus did *not* pray for, namely wealth and position.
3. **marmorei...tecti:** As often in Roman poetry, marble signifies wealth.
prodirem < *prodeo*.
4. **clara...domo:** "famous family"; ablative of cause. *domus* here refers to the family, *tecti* (3) to the building.
5. **renouarent:** lit.: "renew," i.e., by ploughing earth previously fallow. Trans.: "turn over."
multa...iugera: "many acres." A *iugerum*, technically, is about two-thirds of an acre, but often, as here, it is loosely used in the plural of a large tract of land.
7-10. What Lygdamus *did* pray for.
7. **sociarem:** "share."

8. nostra senecta: abstract for concrete. Lit.: "that my old age might....." Trans: "that I, in my old age, might...."
  sinu: "embrace" or "arms" (lit. "bosom").
9. tunc cum: "at the time when...."
  defunctus < *defungor*, "complete, fulfill"; with ablative.
  permenso < *permetior*, "measure out, allot." The participle here is passive in meaning.
10. Lethaea...rate: "on the boat of Lethe." Lethe was a river or spring of the Underworld whose water bestowed forgetfulness on the dead souls who drank from it. Usually the dead cross the river *Acheron* on Charon's boat, but here the poet conflates the two sets of water.
11. grave...pondus: here the subject of *prodest*, as is the whole of the *si* clause in line 12.
12. arva: "fields," but always used of ploughed land.
  findant: "split, cleave," often used of ploughing. The subjunctive expresses a remote future possibility.
13. innixa < *innitor*, "rest on," "be supported by."
  Phrygiis...columnis: "Phrygian" marble, imported from Synnada in Phrygia, was much used for columns, and for the Roman poets it typified the life of luxury. According to Pliny the Elder, it was soaked in wine and heated until it turned red.
14. Taenare...Caryste: both vocatives. Taenarus, a promontory on the southern tip of the Peloponnese, and Carystus, a coastal town in Euboea, were both noted for their marble-quarries.
  tuis...tuis: sc. *columnis*.
15. nemora: though plural, a subject of *prodest*, singular because the closest subject is the singular *domus*. Trees planted in the courtyard of a house signified luxury.
  imitantia: lit.: "imitating." Trans.: "as great as" or "like."
16. aurataeque trabes marmoreumque solum: again subjects of *prodest*.
  trabes: "beams."
  solum: "floor."
17. quidue: sc. *iuuat* (18).
  quae: postponed and governed by *concha* which is the subject of *legitur*. "What is the use of the shell which...." The reference is to pearls, for which the Arabian Gulf or "red" sea (*mare Erythrum*) was celebrated.
18. tincta < *tingo* "dye, stain."
  Sidonio murice: The Phoenician town of Sidon was famed for its purple dye, extracted from the shellfish called the *murex*. Here, as often, the word *murex* is used of the dye itself.
19. et quae praeterea: "and the other things which," a further subject of *iuuat*.

19-20. in illis/inuidia est: lit.: "There is envy in these," i.e., they excite jealousy.
20. falso: adverb, "misguidedly, without justification."
21. non opibus: emphatically positioned: "It is not by riches that...."
22. sua...lege: emphatic: "by rules of its own."
23. mihi: possessive: "Let me have."
paupertas: not destitution, but slender means.
tecum iucunda: "sweet with you."
25. O niveam...lucem: exclamatory accusative: "Oh fortunate day!" *O* in Latin always indicates extreme emotion. *niveus* (lit. "snow-white") is often, like *albus* or *candidus*, the colour of good fortune.
26. mihi: dative of advantage.
felicem...diem: exclamatory accusative.
27. quaecumque uouentur: "Whatever will be offered as vows." *quaecumque* is object of *audiat* (28). For vows, see on line 1.
28. auersa...aure: i.e., with ear turned away and therefore not listening.
non meus...deus: i.e., not on my side, not well-disposed towards me.
29. Lydius aurifer amnis: the "Lydian gold-bearing river" is the Pactolus, a river in Lydia in Asia Minor which was renowned for the large quantities of gold-dust found in its mud.
30. opes: "wealth"; also subject of *iuuant* with *regna* and *Lydius aurifer amnis*.
31. cupiant; liceat: jussives.
paupere cultu: ablative of attendant circumstance: (i.e., ablative absolute without a participle) "with a modest way of life."
32. securo: "carefree, free from anxiety", with *mihi* (31).
frui < *fruor*, "enjoy"; + ablative.
33. adsis: "appear, help me." *adesse* is the word conventionally used, in the subjunctive or imperative, in a prayer requesting help of a god.
faueas < *faueo*, "give ear to, favour"; + dative.
Saturnia: "daughter of Saturn," i.e., Juno.
34. concha...uecta tua: Since she was sea-born, Venus was often represented as using a sea shell as her chariot. uecta: < *uehor*, "be carried," i.e., "ride." (*concha... tua* is instrumental ablative).
Cypria: Venus who, according to the myth, came to Cyprus after her birth from the sea-foam.
35. reditum: i.e., Neaera's return to Lygdamus.
35-36. tristesque sorores/stamina quae ducunt: the fates, often represented as three sisters who spin the threads of destiny.
36. canunt < *cano*, here, as often, "prophesy."

37. uastos amnes: the Underworld, which was often represented as a tractless marsh.
    uastos: "desolate."
38. diues...Orcus: Orcus is the personification of death, equivalent to the Greek Pluto, whose name the Greeks connected etymologically with the word *plutos* ("wealth"). Hence *dives*.
    ignava: i.e., sluggish, slow-moving.
    luridus: "pale, ghastly."

LYGDAMUS 4 ([Tib.] 3.4)

Lygdamus' Nightmare

1. **meliora:** "better omens," i.e., than last night's dream.
    ferant...sint: jussives.
    mihi: dative of disadvantage.
2. **pessima...quies:** trans.: "my troubled sleep."
3. **uani:** "idle." Understand *somni*, but the text may not be sound.
    falsumque avertite visum: "take away your false illusion."
4. **desinite in nobis quaerere uelle fidem:** lit.: "Cease wishing to seek belief in us." Trans.: "Stop trying to win credence by using me."
5. **diui** = *di*.
    uera monent: "give reliable prophecies." *vera* is "internal" accusative (Woodcock §16).
    nuntia < *nuntius-a-um*, "giving warning (of things to come)." Nominative neuter plural in agreement with *exta* (6).
6. **Tuscis...uiris:** dative of the agent, often used with passive participles. The *haruspices*, a class of diviners, were of Etruscan origin.
    exta: "animal entrails" (the upper internal organs of an animal).
    probata: "examined, inspected."
7. **fallaci...nocte:** ablative of time. *fallaci* ("fraudulent" or "deceitful") because things are less clear at night.
    ludunt: "play tricks, deceive."
    temeraria: "that come at random, that occur fortuitously."
8. **falsa timere iubent:** "order (us) to fear untrue things," i.e., "inspire false fears."
9. **†natum...maturas†:** The text is corrupt and cannot be satisfactorily restored.
10. **farre...sale:** "with meal and salt." i.e., *mola salsa*, a mixture of salt and spelt which was frequently used in sacrifice.
    saliente: lit. "leaping," i.e., "crackling, sputtering."
    placant: "try to avert." Plural after the collective subject *hominum genus* (9).

11. utcumque est: "whatever the truth be, whatever the facts are."
uera moneri: sc. *solent* (12). On *uera*, see note on line 5.
12. mendaci somno: "the deceptions of sleep" (lit. "deceptive sleep"); dative with *credere*.
13. efficiat uanos: jussive: "let [Lucina] render ineffectual..."
Lucina: Juno, goddess of marriage.
14. immeritum: sc. *me*.
pertimuisse uelit: lit. "let her wish that I have been terrified in vain." Trans.: "let her decree that my fears were unjustified."
15. si mea...mens...obnoxia: "if my heart is not disposed to..."
16. laesit: "offended."
17-18. aetherium.../mundum: "the firmament of heaven."
**emensa < *emetior* "traverse, pass over."
18. caeruleo...amne: the ocean, i.e., night (often represented as having a chariot and horses) had already passed.
rotas: the wheels of the chariot drawn by her four chariot-horses (*quadrigis* [17]).
19. sopierat < *sopio*, "overcome with sleep."
menti...aegrae: dative of advantage after *utilis*.
20. sollicitas...domos: "houses that are filled with care."
deficit: "fails, loses his power."
21. summo...ab ortu: "from his highest rising," i.e., when the sun was fully risen.
Phoebus: Apollo, god of the sun.
22. languentis: sc. *mei*. Trans.: "my drooping eyes (*lumina*)."
23. hic: "at this point."
redimitus tempora: internal accusative. Trans.: "his temples surrounded...."
24. est visus: sc. *mihi*, "seemed to me." Trans.: "I dreamed a young man...set foot."
nostra...sede: "in my house"; ablative of place where.
25. illo: ablative of comparison.
quicquam formosius: neuter; "anything more beautiful."
26. humanum: genitive plural; "of human beings."
nec uidet: "has not seen," i.e., has not in the past and still does not today.
27. Apollo is always represented by the poets as a young god with long hair.
28. Syrio...rore: lit.: "with Syrian dew," i.e., Syrian perfume. Syria was famous for its exotic spices and perfumes (especially spikenard).
myrrhea...coma: "his light-brown hair."
29. candor: "a fair complexion."
erat: sc. *ei*: "he had."

Latonia Luna: Diana, daughter of Latona, was identified with the moon.
30. **color...purpureus:** "a rosy tinge."
31. **ut:** "as."
    iuueni...marito: dative of the agent (see on 6).
    deducta: "led in marriage" < *deduco* is the technical word used for taking a new bride in procession to the husband's house.
32. **teneras...genas:** Lit. "is discoloured as to her tender cheeks" (i.e., blushes).
    ore rubente: ablative absolute. Trans.: "and her face turns red."
33. **et cum:** "or when."
    amarantis: "with amaranths" (richly coloured flowers, predominantly purple, which are long in withering and so appear often in ancient poetry as emblems of immortality).
34. **autumno:** temporal ablative: "in autumn."
35. **uidebatur:** See on 24.
    talis < *talus*, "ankle"; dative with *inludere*, "to play around."
37. **artis opus rarae:** in apposition to *garrula...lyra* (38).
    fulgens testudine et auro: also describing *garrula...lyra* (38).
    testudine: "with tortoise-shell."
38. **laeua...parte:** ablative of place where: "on his left side."
39. **primum ueniens:** i.e., on his arrival.
    modulatus: "playing." N.B.: Past participles of deponent verbs often represent action *contemporaneous* with the action of the main verb (Woodcock §103).
40. **felices:** of poetry, song, etc. "felicitous," "elegant," "well-turned."
41. **fuerant...locuti:** = *locuti erant*.
42. **edidit:** "he uttered."
43. **deum** = *deorum*.
    casto...poetae: "a holy poet." (Poets were commonly thought to enjoy divine protection).
    rite: "justly, rightly."
44. **Pierides:** the Muses (see on Lygdamus 1.5).
45. **doctaeque sorores:** i.e., the Muses.
46. **dicere:** "to declare, to prophesy."
    norunt: abbreviated form of *noverunt*.< *nosco*, here "know how (to)."
    hora sequens: i.e., the future.
47. **at mihi:** because Apollo is the god of prophecy.
48. **euentura:** i.e., "things that will happen."
    posse uidere: "the ability to foresee."
49. **non fallax...uates:** in apposition to *ego*.
    accipe: "listen to."

50. quamque...ferar: The clause is dependent on *accipe* (49) and *quam* is to be taken closely with *uero...ore*, a descriptive ablative. "And [hear] of what truthful voice I, the Cynthian god, am reported to be."
  Cynthius: "belonging to Mt. Cynthus," on Delos, on which Apollo and his sister Diana were reputedly born.
51-61. The sentence could be broken up in translation. 51-56, all in apposition to *Neaera* (57), may be made a main clause. "Neaera is more dear to you than any daughter to her mother etc."
  tantum cara tibi quantum nec: "as dear to you as no daughter to her mother," i.e., more dear.
52. cupido: "passionate."
  bella: very rare in elegy because it is a "low" word, i.e., one which belongs to common speech. The normal "literary" word is *pulcher*.
53-4. qua...quae: Neaera.
53. sollicitas...uotis: "you torment with vows." On *uota* see on 3.1.
54. tibi: dative of disadvantage.
  securos: "carefree, without anxiety."
56. uanum...fallit: The subject is Neaera, and *vanum* (sc. *te*) is proleptic; "cheats and deceives you with dreams at night."
57. celebrata: "made famous."
59. diuersasque suas...curas: "its own private (lit. "separate," i.e., other than with Lygdamus) love affairs."
  impia: "cheating, deceitful" (in the context of love).
60. nec gaudet...nupta: i.e., *nec gaudet se nuptam esse*.
61. nec fidum femina nomen: sc. *est*. *nomen = gens*.
62. a pereat...si qua: "a curse upon any woman who...."
63. illis: possessive dative.
64. cum multa...prece: "with many an entreaty."
  bracchia tende: the gesture of supplication.
65-66. docuit...docuit: "gnomic" (i.e., generalising) perfect. Trans: "Love teaches a person...."
67. me quondam: *me* emphatically placed to give an example from personal experience; "That I myself once..." According to the Alexandrian poet Callimachus and others, Apollo served Admetus because he was in love with him (as here); in other versions his service was a punishment from Zeus.
  pauisse < *pasco*.
68. inuanum...iocum: *in* expresses purpose; "to provide idle amusement."
69. gaudere + ablative: "to take pleasure (in)."
  sonora: "harmonious, sweet-toned."

70. similes chordis...sonos: lit.: "to utter with my voice sounds similar to the lyre-strings." Trans.: "to sing lyrics in tune with the strings."
71. perlucenti < *perluceo*, "let light in:" *perlucenti...avena*, a reed pierced with holes (a rustic instrument, contrasted with the lyre). Apollo abandoned the lyre for the rustic pipe (*auena*) to please Admetus.
74. dominam: the conventional term for the beloved in Roman Elegy.
coniugiumque ferum: "a cruel union" or perhaps, less likely, "a cruel partner."
75. adhibere: "to employ, avail yourself of."
querellas: not "complaints" but "entreaties" (as often in the language of love).
77. uera: accusative after *canunt*; see on line 5.
79. hoc...coniugium: See on #74.
Delius: i.e., Apollo, who was born on Delos.
80. felix hoc: sc. *coniugio:* "fortunate in this union...."
81. dixit, et: a common narrative formula. Subordinate in translating: "When he had said this...."
ignauus: "lethargic, listless."
82. a: "alas!"
ne possim: "May I never have occasion to, live to...."
83. tibi...(esse) contraria vota: indirect statement after *crediderim*.
uotis: sc. *meis*; dative after *contraria*, "opposed to."
uota: here simply "hopes," "desires."
85. uasti...ponti: "the desolate sea."
86. Chimaera: a fire-breathing monster, part lion, part snake and part goat.
87. redimitus terga: See on *Lygdamus* 2.11. The reference is to the "hound of hell," Cerberus.
88. cui tres sunt linguae: "who has three tongues...."
89. uirgineam...figuram: "internal" accusative with passive participle *succincta*: "her virgin body hemmed with...." Scylla was a half-human sea-monster sometimes confused or conflated (as by Lygdamus) with the young daughter of Nisus, king of Megara, whom she betrayed when she fell in love with Minos who was besieging the city. *uirgineam* therefore has point.
90. te conceptam...tulit: Latin tends to subordinate ideas that are expressed by coordinate constructions in English. Translate: "conceived and bore you."
91. Scythiae...Syrtis: proverbially distant and inhospitable places. Scythia was an area north and north-east of the Black Sea, the Syrtes two sandy flats on the coast of N. Africa.
92. duris: "cruel-hearted people;" dative of agent.

94.. **quo:** ablative of comparison. "A father than whom none is more amiable," i.e., a supremely amiable father.
95. **in melius:** "into (something) better."
somnia: plural for singular.
96. **inrita ferre:** sc. *somnia*; proleptic: "to sweep it away unfulfilled" (i.e., so it becomes unfulfilled).

LYGDAMUS 5 ([Tib.] 3.5)

A letter from Lygdamus, who is ill, to his holidaying friends

1. **uos:** emphatically positioned.
Etruscis: Etruria was famous for its hot-spring spas.
manat < *mano*, "flow, run."
2. **sub aestiuum...Canem:** "at the approach of the dog-star's heat," i.e., from the time of the morning rising of Sirius, late in July, which began the "Dog Days," the hottest period of the year.
non adeunda: "that should not be visited."
3. **nunc:** "but now" (in this season).
Baiarum...lymphis: Baiae, west of Naples, was the most renowned watering-place in Italy.
proxima: "next to," i.e., "second best to."
sacris: from Hercules who was supposed to have driven the cattle of Geryon past Baiae.
4. **se...remittit:** "thaws."
purpureo uere: temporal ablative; "in rosy spring-time."
5. **nigram...horam:** "my hour of darkness," i.e., death.
6. **immerito:** dative adjective, with *iuueni*. Trans.: "for I am innocent."
parce + infinitive = *noli* + infinitive, "do not...."
7. **nulli temeranda uirorum:** to be taken with *sacra* (8); *temeranda*: "to be desecrated."
8. **audax:** with *ego* (7) and adverbial in force. Trans.: "I have not recklessly...."
laudandae...deae: i.e., the *Bona Dea*, a mystery goddess whose rites were forbidden to men.
9-10. **mea...dextera:** nominative.
9. **infecit:** "poisoned."
10. **trita:** "powdered, pulverised"; < *tero*.
11. **nos:** i.e., *ego*.
templis: dative after compound *admovimus*.
12. **facta nefanda:** "abominable activities, immoral conduct."

13. nec...mentis: "nor, contemplating profanity in (lit. "of") a sick mind...."
14. impia: "blasphemous."
    in adversos...deos: "against the gods [who were] opposed [to my wishes]."
15. cani: sc. *capilli*.
16. tardo: "limping."
    curua: i.e., age that makes one stoop.
17. uidere = *viderunt*.
18. cecidit fato...pari: "met the same end." Hirtius and Pansa, consuls for the year 43 B.C., were killed in the civil war at Mutina during that year. The same line occurs in Ovid (*Tristia* 4.10.6). See Introduction.
19. crescentibus uuis: ablative of separation (Woodcock §41[8]).
20. modo nata: i.e., that have just taken shape as fruit.
    mala...manu: "with a cruel hand."
21. parcite: sc. *mihi*.
    pallentes: See on *Lygdamus* 1.28.
    quicumque: with *dei* (22).
22 sortiti: sc. *sunt*: "who have been allotted...."
    tertia: In the primeval allotment of kingdoms, Heaven fell to Jupiter, the Sea to Neptune and the Underworld, the "third" kingdom, to Pluto.
23. olim: can refer to the future, as here; "some time later on."
24. Lethaeamque ratem: See on *Lygdamus* 3.10.
    Cimmerios: not the historical Cimmerians, but a fabulous people who appear in Homer's *Odyssey* near the land of the dead.
25. rugosa...senecta: "with wrinkled old age."
27. utinam + subjunctive: "I wish that...."
    uano...aestu: "by an imaginary fever."
28. quinos...dies: accusative of extent or duration.
29. uobis: dative of the agent, occasionally found in poetry, to be taken with both *celebrantur* and *pellitur* (30).
    celebrantur: "are frequented."
30. facilis...pellitur: "is easily parted."
    lenta...manu: "by your gentle (swimming) stroke."
31. et: postponed.
    nostri: genitive of *nos*: "of me."
32. erimus: "I shall survive."
    fuisse uelint: "decide that my life be over." *Fuisse* is a true perfect signifying that the action (here "being" or "living") is over.
33. nigras: the colour associated with the Underworld.
    promittite: i.e., as a *uotum* (see on *Lygdamus* 3.1) for Lygdamus' recovery.

34. lactis pocula mixta mero: A mixture of milk and wine was a common sacrificial offering.

LYGDAMUS 6 ([Tib.] 3.6)

Lygdamus, at a symposium, wishes to drown his sorrows.

1. **Candide:** "fair, beautiful."
   Liber: Bacchus, Dionysus.
   ades: "appear." See on Lygdamus 3.33.
   sic sit tibi: "so may you have, on this condition may you have."
   Such a reciprocal wish is common in Latin prayers.
2. **tempora:** "temples."
   uincta < *uincio.*
3. **et ipse:** "in person."
   patera: i.e., of wine.
4. **cecidit** < *cado.* Trans.: "been overthrown."
5. **care puer:** Lygdamus turns to the slave who serves the wine.
   madeant < *madeo.* "be wet," i.e., "be filled."
   generoso: "choice, vintage."
6. **prona...manu:** "with hand tilted" (i.e., to pour more).
   Falerna: often cited by the poets as a typical vintage wine, from northern Campania.
7. **durum curae genus:** *curae* is vocative, with *durum...genus* in apposition to it.
   labores: "troubles."
8. **fulserit** < *fulgeo* Perfect subjunctive, expressing a wish that something may prove to have happened; i.e., by the day's end may the sun have been shining all day.
   alitibus: i.e., swans, often associated with Apollo.
9. **proposito:** "my intention," i.e., to get drunk.
   dulces...amici: vocative.
10. **me duce:** ablative of attendant circumstance (ablative absolute without a participle). Lygdamus is to be the *arbiter bibendi*, the "party-leader" who decides the strength (i.e., proportion of wine to water) and quantities to be drunk by the company, who must try to keep up with him.
    neget ... se comitem: "refuse his companionship."
11. **certamen:** See on line 10.
12. **fallat:** jussive.
    tecto < *tego,* "cover, conceal."
    dolo: i.e., infidelity.
13. **ille...deus:** i.e., Amor.

facit mites: "calms, softens."
14. contudit...misit: "gnomic" perfects.
misit in arbitrium: "puts him at the mercy of...."
17. haec...maiora: "internal" accusatives. Trans.: "Love has this power and more."
17-18. Bacchi munera: i.e., wine.
18. uestrum < *uos*; partitive genitive after *quem*.
sicca: "empty" or perhaps "sober."
19. convenit ex aequo: "meets on equal terms;" i.e., is not hostile towards.
in illis: "towards those."
20. una: adverb: "simultaneously, at the same time."
21. The line is corrupt but the message clearly is the opposite of 19-20: the god is hostile to non-drinkers.
22. qui: Understand *ille*.
23. quales...poenas...minetur: "what sort of punishments he threatens"; indirect question governed by *docet* (24).
his: i.e., those unsympathetic to Bacchus.
qualis quantusque: "the character and power of the god who threatens (i.e., the *poenas*)."
24. Cadmeae...docet: i.e., the story of Pentheus, persecutor of Dionysus, torn apart by Bacchanals, including Agave, mother of Pentheus, who in their Bacchic frenzy took him for a lion.
Cadmeae: Agave was Cadmus' daughter, but *Cadmeus, -a, -um* is a poetic synonym for *Thebanus*.
praeda: perhaps specifically Pentheus' head, carried triumphantly by his mother Agave after his killing.
25. illaque: sc. Neaera.
si qua est: "if anyone."
26. quid ualeat...ira: indirect question dependent on *sentiat*; "feel the power of a slighted god's anger."
27. temeraria: "reckless."
28. et: postponed.
diripienda ferant: "carry (them) to be torn apart," i.e., to destruction.
29. mei: objective genitive of *ego*.
30. candida: See on *Lygdamus* 3.25.
31. securae: "that banishes cares."
reddamus tempora: jussive; "let us devote our time to...."
32. una serena: sc. *dies* (usually masculine, but often feminine when reference is to a specific day).
34. tristi...mente: ablative of attendant circumstance; "when the heart is sad."

35. nec bene...componitur: "is poorly fabricated."
36. sollicitis: ablative of origin: "from those with cares," i.e., drunkenness should accompany joyfulness, not sadness.
37. infelix: nominative, with adverbial force; "wretchedly, unhappily."
   turpes...curae: vocative.
38. Lenaeus: Greek title of Bacchus ("belonging to the wine-press"). Trans.: "Father Bacchus."
39. Gnosia: lit.: "woman of Cnossus," i.e., Ariadne.
   Thesaeae...periuria linguae: i.e., the false oaths uttered by Theseus.
40. ignoto...mari: "to an unfamiliar sea." Ariadne was deserted by Theseus on the island of Naxos.
41. doctus...Catullus: an adjective frequently applied to Catullus (and other poets). Perhaps here there is a particular point to it in that the poem referred to, Catullus 64, is much indebted in style and content to Hellenistic Greek poetry.
   Minoi: vocative; Ariadne's father was King Minos.
42. impia: "wicked" because Theseus repaid Ariachne for her services to him (helping him kill the Minotaur) by deserting her (so *ingrati*).
43. uos: i.e., the drinking-companions of Lygdamus.
   felix: sc. *es*.
44. posse cauere tuom: "to be able to avoid your own (sc. *dolorem*)."
45. capiant: "captivate."
   pendentia...collo: "clinging to (lit. "hanging from") your neck."
46. sordida lingua: "avaricious tongue."
47. fallax: nominative and adverbial in force; "although she has sworn falsely."
48. suam: because each woman has her Juno, or tutelary deity, as each man has his Genius.
50. inrita: proleptic.
51. quid: "why?"
   totiens: grammatically with *conqueror*, but also qualifying *fallacis*.
53. quam uellem: "How I would like...."
   longas...noctes: accusative of extent.
55. perfida: vocative.
   †**nobis...merenti**†: The text is corrupt, but the meaning is evidently that Lygdamus still loves Neaera despite her perfidy.
57. Naida: a naiad or water nymph, i.e., the wine and water should be mixed, ready for drinking. The accusative in *a* is Greek, often used with Greek proper names by Roman authors.
   o: See on *Lygdamus* 3.25.
58. Marcia lympha: i.e., water brought to Rome by the aqueduct known as the *Aqua Marcia* constructed by Q. Marcius Rex (praetor B.C.

144). It originated in the Paelignian range, east of Rome, and was renowned for its purity.
59. nostrae conuiuia mensae: "the banquet found at my table."
60. ignotum...torum: "a stranger's bed."
63. tempora: See on *Lygdamus* 4.23.
64. debueram: "I should have."
    sertis implicuisse comas: "to set a garland on my hair," the traditional custom at a symposium.

THE GARLAND OF SULPICIA 1
([Tib.] 3.8 = 4.2)

Introduction to the Garland: Sulpicia on March 1st

1. est tibi culta: "is dressed up in your honour." Sulpicia is dressed up for the *Matronalia* (see on *Lygdamus* 1.1).
    tuis...kalendis: Mars is addressed because the festival falls on the first day of *his* month.
2. spectatum: supine expressing purpose.
    ipse ueni: "come in person"
3. hoc: accusative, referring to the offense (i.e., coming from heaven and leaving Venus)
    caueto: "future" imperative. See Woodcock §126, 1.
4. tibi miranti: dative of disadvantage; "See your arms do not fall, to your shame (*turpiter*), as you look in amazement."
5. illius: emphatically positioned; "it is from *her* eyes ...."
    uult: The subject is *Amor* (6).
    exurere: "to inflame with passion."
6. *Amor* is frequently represented as carrying a torch. Here, to match the eyes, he has two.
7. quoquo uestigia mouit: Translate simply "wherever she goes."
8. componit < *compono*, here "adorns, beautifies."
    Decor: "elegance, beauty." Of course, a personification.
9. fusis...capillis: descriptive ablative. *decet* (impersonal) + infin. *esse*: lit. "it is becoming (sc. for her) to be with hair dishevelled."
10. compsit < *como*, "arrange, do" (of hair).
    ueneranda: i.e., she commands veneration, like the god himself.
11. urit: Understand *omnes* or *homines* as object.
    Tyria...palla: descriptive ablative; "in a cloak of Tyrian purple." Tyre was famous for its crimson dye, produced from a shell-fish.
    uoluit procedere: "she has decided to go out."
12. niuea: ablative (of respect) with *ueste*.
13. talis...Vertumnus: "Just so ... Vertumnus ..."

Vertumnus: an Etruscan god associated by the Romans with the changing seasons (cf. *uertere*, to turn) and so with change in general; hence his "thousand modes of dress."

14. mille decenter habet: "and wears a thousand handsomely," i.e., "and is handsome in a thousand."

15-16. digna est cui....det...Tyros: "she...deserves to have Tyre offer her..." For the relative and subjunctive after *dignus*: see Woodcock §158.

16. bis: Double-dyeing meant the garment was very expensive.

17. bene olentibus aruis: ablative of place where; "in his fragrant fields."

18. odoratae...segetis: objective genitive dependent on *cultor*.

Arabs: See on *Lygdamus* 2.24.

19. niger: with *Indus* (20)

Rubro: For the "red" sea, see on *Lygdamus* 3.17.

20. proximus Eois...aquis: "living next to the waters of the East."

Eois: See on *Lygdamus* 2.24.

21. hanc: emphatically positioned: "It is of her you must sing...."

uos: The author addresses both the Muses (*Pierides*) and Apollo (*Phoebe*, 22).

Pierides: See on *Lygdamus* 1.5.

22. testudinea: ablative (of respect) with *lyra:* "veneered with tortoise-shell, with its tortoise-shell veneer."

23. sollemne sacrum: "sacred rite, holy ritual."

multos...in annos: "for many years."

24. uestro...choro: ablative after *dignior*: "more deserving of your musical praise (*choro*)."

GARLAND 2
([Tib.] 3.9 = 4.3).

Sulpicia to her beloved Cerinthus who has gone hunting.

1-2. seu quis...colis...aper: Take *aper* as vocative and in translating omit *quis* (which is used to show that the address is to *any* boar, not a specific one): "boar, whether you frequent ...."

colis < *colo*, "inhabit, live in, frequent."

3. sit: jussive. The subject is the infinitive *acuisse*: "let it not be yours to have whetted your teeth," i.e., do not whet your teeth. Traditionally the most dangerous of hunting animals, the boar is often represented as sharpening his teeth in preparation for the fight.

4. custos: in apposition to *Amor*.

Two or more lines may have been lost from the text after line 4.

5. **Delia:** Diana, goddess of the hunt, who was born on Delos (see on *Lygdamus* 4.50).
   cura: instrumental ablative with *uenandi*; "by his love of hunting."
6. **canes:** an indispensable part of the ancient hunter's equipment.
7. **mens:** here, "insanity."
   densos: "thickly-treed."
   indagine: "with a cordon" (of hunstmen, who would encircle the quarry with nets).
8. **claudentem...uelle:** accusative and infinitive dependent on *quis furor...quae mens*: "what madness it is...to wish to...by encircling (*claudentem*)."
   teneras: conventional epithet in Elegy applied to the lover's physique and various parts of his body (e.g., hands, fingers, cheeks, feet, etc.) - he is inevitably pale, weak and unused to physical exertion. It is also frequently applied to the girl.
10. **notare:** "to scratch, graze."
11. **liceat:** sc. *mihi esse.*
12. **ipsa ego...feram:** "I will carry ... with my very own hands" (emphatic because this is a male slave's task and Sulpicia is a freeborn woman).
    retia: used by the cordon (line 7 above) who closed in on the animal.
15. **lux mea:** conventional term of endearment in elegy, "My darling."
16 **arguar...concubuisse:** "I am accused of having lain with you ....." ("Accused" because she is freeborn girl and therefore such liaisons are forbidden).
17. **ueniat:** subjunctive dependent on *licet* (trans. "although") with *aper* (18) as subject.
    abibit < *abire*, which often has the sense (as here) of "getting off" or "getting away" with something.
18. **ueneris cupidae:** "our passionate love-making."
19. **sit:** jussive.
    lege Dianae: "in accordance with the rules of Diana" (goddess of the hunt *and* chastity).
21-22. **quaecumque...incidat:** "let any woman who...."
    subrepit: lit.: "creeps up on," i.e., "has designs upon."
22. **diripienda:** gerundive expressing purpose ("to be torn apart [by them]").
24. **celer:** adverbial in force; "quickly."
    in nostros...sinus: plural for singular, "to my embrace."

GARLAND 3
([Tib.] 3.10 = 4.4)

The poet prays to Apollo, on Cerinthus' behalf, to deliver Sulpicia from sickness.

1. **Huc ades:** formulaic. See on *Lygdamus* 3.33.
   tenerae: See on *Garland* 2.8. Dative after compound verb *expelle*.
   morbos: plural for singular.
2. **huc ades:** Such repetition is a regular feature of Roman prayers.
   Phoebe: Apollo, god of healing as well as music and archery. See on *Lygdamus* 4.27.
3. **nec te...pigebit:** impersonal, but translate: "you'll not regret...."
4. **formosae:** dative after compound *applicuisse*.
   medicas: "healing."
5. **effice ne + *subj*.:** "See to it that...not...."
   macies: "emaciation, wasting disease."
6. **informis...color:** i.e., the "unsightly" color of illness.
7. **mali:** partitive genitive. Translate: "whatever misfortune."
8. **in pelagus:** "out to sea."
   euehat: jussive. A wish that misfortune be directed elsewhere is a standard feature of prayer.
9. **sapores:** lit. "tastes," here "juices" or "medicines." For attraction into the nominative, see on *Lygdamus* 2.17.
10. **fessa:** "ailing," often used of sickness.
11. **iuuenem:** i.e. Cerinthus.
    fata: "death."
12. **uotaque:** See on *Lygdamus* 3.1.
13. **quod langueat:** subjunctive because *Cerinthus'* reason for his harsh words against the gods is given (see Woodcock §240), but this cannot be satisfactorily rendered in English. Translate simply: "because she is failing."

21-22. These lines appear in the manuscripts after line 20, but it is generally agreed that this is the result of a scribal error and that the author's original text had these placed after line 16.

21. **lacrimis erit aptius uti:** "It will be more appropriate to resort to (*uti*) tears...."
22. **tristior...tibi:** "annoyed with you, exasperated with you." As often, the comparative here expresses the idea of a *considerable amount*, which can be translated in English by the simple adjective.

17-18. **te solum...cogitat:** "She has you only in her mind" (lit.: "she thinks you only with herself").

18. credula turba: i.e., Sulpicia's other admirers, each thinking (wrongly) that he has a chance to win her love.
19. laus magna tribuetur: Here, as often in prayers, the god is given a selfish reason for granting the prayer.
20. restituisse: "to have revived, restored to life."
23-4. debita...uterque: "when they (i.e., Cerinthus and Sulpicia) will joyfully compete with each other (*certatim*) to repay the vows they owe (*debita*)."
23. debita reddet: See on *Lygdamus* 3.1.
26. optabunt...quisque: The verb is usually singular with *quisque* but sometimes, as here, it is "attracted" into the plural by the plural sense of the word.

GARLAND 4
([Tib.] 3.11 = 4.5)

The birthday of Cerinthus

1. **Qui:** Take *dies* as the antecedent.
   hic: sc. *dies*, i.e., today.
2. **festos:** sc. *dies*: "feast-days, holidays."
3. **nouum (seruitium [4]):** i.e., hitherto unknown to them. The "slavery" of one partner to another (usually the lover to the girl) is a recurring theme of Roman Elegy.
   cecinere < *cano*, 3rd person plural: "foretold."
5. **uror:** often in love poetry of the flames of passion.
   iuuat: sc. *me*.
6. **de:** i.e., a fire "caught from" Sulpicia, but translate "for me."
7. **adsit:** paratactic, dependent on *rogo* (8).
   per te dulcissima furta: "(I beg) you in the name of the secret pleasures of our love." *te* is the object of *rogo* (8); *per* governs *dulcissima furta* (see on *Lygdamus* 1.15).
8. **Geniumque:** The *Genius* of a man was his inner spirit (see on *Lygdamus* 6.48) and was always honoured (as here) on his birthday.
9. **tura:** "frankincense," often used in religious ceremonies. Plural for singular.
   faueto: future imperative, "be indulgent to."
11. **suspirat +** *acc.*: "sighs with longing for...."
12. **precor:** parenthetic.
13. **iniusta:** "unfair," i.e., making the love of one them stronger than the other's.
    aeque: can be taken either with *seruiat* or with *uihctus* (14).

14. uinctus...uincla: The idea of "chains of love," a notion linked to the *seruitium amoris* (see on line 3), is common in Elegy.
15. potius: "preferably."
   teneamur uterque: For the plural verb with *uterque*, see on Garland 3.26.
16. nulla queat...quam...dies: "which no passage of time could..." *queat* is generic subjunctive (subjunctive of characteristic): Woodcock §155.
   soluisse: The perfect infinitive emphasises the completion of the action, but this cannot be rendered satisfactorily in English.
17. idem: neuter singular.
   tectius: "more discreetly, less openly."
19. Natalis = the *genius* of lines 8-9.
   deus: in apposition to the subject (you): "being divine."
20. clamne: *ne* here introduces an indirect question (Woodcock §182).

GARLAND 5
([Tib.] 3.12 = 4.6)

Sulpicia's birthday.

1. Iuno: the female tutelary deity, corresponding to the male's *Genius*, and so appropriately addressed on a birthday.
   sanctos: transferred epithet; it is really the *tus* which is holy.
2. tenera: See on *Garland* 2.8.
   docta puella: i.e., a girl cultivated in literature and the arts, like Propertius' Cynthia, Tibullus' Delia and Ovid's Corinna.
3-4. tibi...tibi...tuos: Such repetition of the second person, with no connectives, is a regular feature of ancient prayers.
   conspicienda: "for all to behold."
5-6. quidem...tamen: The force of the opposition "on the one hand, on the other" is difficult to render elegantly in English. Translate: "While she makes you the pretext (lit. "relegates to you the reasons") for her attire, there is however someone (i.e., Cerinthus)....".
6. placuisse: For the perfect, see on Garland 4.16.
   uelit: potential: "she would like...."
7. neu quis = *et ne quis*.
   diuellat: jussive.
8. uincla: See on *Garland* 4.14.
9. compones: sc. *illos*. "Thus you will make a good match, pair them off well."
   ullae: for *ulli*, an unprecedented usage (though *nullae* is occasionally found).

10. seruire: epexegetic infinitive dependent on *dignior* (which is to be taken with both *ille* [9] and *illa* [10]). See Woodcock §26. Translate: "no other girl is he more suited to serve, no other man she." For the *servitium amoris*, see on Garland 4.3.

11. cupidos: sc. *illos:* "the eager lovers."

custos: a guardian, employed especially to protect married women and (as here) unmarried girls.

13. perlucida: "radiant, resplendent" (possibly, but less likely, "transparent").

14. fit libo: *facere* (passive *fieri*) + ablative: sometimes means (as here) "to sacrifice [with]." So "sacrifice is made to you with a cake" or "a cake is sacrificed to you."

15. et: postponed.

16. tacita...mente: "silently" or "in her heart."

18. sana: i.e., free from love for Cerinthus. Love is frequently represented as a disease or sickness in Roman Elegy.

19. The line as it stands is corrupt. Ignore the first three words and translate from *veniet*.

20. iam uetus (*amor*): "by now well-established."

adsit (uotis): i.e., still exist when her next birthday prayers are made.

SULPICIA 1 ([Tib.] 3.13 = 4.7)

Sulpicia confesses her love.

1-2. qualem...magis: The subject of the clause is *fama* and *pudori* is predicative dative (i.e., dative of purpose) (Woodcock §68). Translate as new sentence: "The rumour that I had concealed it would cause me greater shame...."

3. exorata: "persuaded."

Cytherea: Venus to whom Cythera, an island off Cape Malea in the Peloponnese, was sacred.

Camenis: "poetry." The Camenae were native Roman goddesses identified with the Greek Muses.

4. sinum: "embrace, arms."

5. exoluit < *ex(s)olvo*.

narret: The subject is *si quis* (6).

6. sua: sc. *gaudia*.

7. signatis: "sealed," (with wax and a signet ring). The past participle is emphatically placed and separated from its noun *tabellis*; i.e., Sulpicia does not seek secrecy for her avowal of love and is prepared to send *unsealed* letters.

8. **me legat ut nemo etc**: goes closely with *signatis*. Her sealing of the tablets would be an attempt to prevent someone from reading the poetry before Cerinthus does.
   quam meus ante = *antequam meus* (sc. *puer*).
9. **peccasse**: *Peccare* is often used in elegy of sexual encounters.
10. **taedet**: sc. *me*.
    cum...fuisse: *Esse cum* is used in erotic contexts of sexual contact (cf. "be with" in English).
    ferar: jussive subjunctive; "let me be said" or, better, "let it be said that I...."

SULPICIA 2
([Tib.] 3.14 = 4.8)

Sulpicia's birthday.

1. **rure molesto**: ablative of place where.
2. **tristis**: with *qui...agendus*, and adverbial ("must be miserably spent.")
3. **dulcius**: nominative neuter, agreeing with *quid*.
   villa: i.e., a house in the country.
   sit: potential.
4. **Arretino**: i.e., of Arretium, a town in Etruria some 100 miles north of Rome; ablative of place where.
   frigidus amnis: Understand *aptus sit*. The "stream" is probably the upper reaches of the Arno.
   Messalla: See Introduction.
5. **mei**: objective genitive, "(over-anxious) on my behalf."
   quiescas: jussive subjunctive instead of imperative. "Relax!"
   Non tempestiuae: sc. *sunt*.
   propinque: vocative: "my kinsman." But an odd way to address Messalla, and the text might be corrupt.
7. **animum sensusque**: "my heart and my emotions."
8. **arbitrio...esse meo**: to live "according to my own judgement." i.e., "to be independent."
   quam: i.e., Sulpicia. Object of *sinit*.
   uis: sc. *amoris*.

SULPICIA 3
([Tib.] 3.15 = 4.9)

The journey cancelled.

1. **scis:** Presumably Cerinthus.
   ex animo: "from the heart."
   sublatum: sc. *esse.*; < *tollo*.
   puellae: "of your girl." Sulpicia is, of course, referring to herself in the third person.
2. **natali...tuo:** temporal ablative. Perhaps *suo* should be read.
   Romae: locative.
   licet: sc. *ei*, referring to Sulpicia herself.
3. **omnibus...nobis:** dative of the agent with *agatur*. To avoid awkwardness, translate as active: "Let us all celebrate...."
4. **qui:** with *dies* (3).
   nec opinanti...tibi: i.e., Cerinthus. Dative of advantage. The surprise, of course, is not that the birthday is coming, but that it is to be spent at Rome.

SULPICIA 4
([Tib.] 3.16 = 4.10)

Sulpicia has learned of Cerinthus' infidelity.

1. **gratum est...quod:** Understand *mihi*; "I am grateful that...." Sulpicia is, of course, sarcastic.
   multum: object of *permittis* (2). The meaning is that Cerinthus is "taking liberties."
2. **ne...cadam:** dependent on *securus*; "unconcerned that I may be humiliated...."
3. **sit tibi cura:** jussive, and sarcastic.
   togae: objective genitive. Prostitutes were often dressed in the *toga*, whereas married women wore the long robe called the *stola*.
3-4. **pressumque quasillo scortum:** sc. *sit potius* (understood from *sit...potior*). "And let the whore loaded down with her woolbasket be preferred to...."
4. **Serui:** Seruius Sulpicius (see Introduction).
5. **pro nobis:** "royal plural," or perhaps a real plural, referring to Cerinthus and Sulpicia.
   quibus: Understand *ei* as antecedent.

dolori: predicative dative, with *illa...maxima causa* as subject of *est* and *quibus* as possessive dative. Translate: "whose greatest sorrow is that...."
6. cedam: i.e., that Sulpicia play "second fiddle" to a mistress of Cerinthus' who is of low birth (*ignoto...toro*).

SULPICIA 5
([Tib.] 3.17 = 4.11)

Sulpicia sick.

1. **tuae puellae:** i.e., Sulpicia herself.
   pia cura: "dutiful concern." It was a friend's duty (*officium*), and so by extension a lover's, to visit a friend (lover) when he/she was ill.
2. **fessa:** See on *Garland* 3.10.
   calor: i.e., a fever.
4. **optarim** = *optauerim*, "potential" perfect subjunctive, often used instead of the present with no observable difference in meaning. "I would...wish."
5. **prosit:** potential.
6. **lento pectore:** "with unfeeling heart."

SULPICIA 6
([Tib.] 3.18 = 4.12)

Sulpicia apologises to Cerinthus.

1. **Ne...sim:** negative jussive.
   feruida cura: complement to *sim*.
2. **ac:** "as," to be taken closely with *aeque* (1).
3. **tota...iuuenta:** temporal ablative.
   stulta: nominative and adverbial in force, "stupidly."
4. **cuius:** genitive dependent on *paenituisse* (< *paenitet*).
   fatear: potential subjunctive; "for which I could express more regret."
5. **quam:** take closely with *magis* (4).
   quod: postponed, introducing the action which Sulpicia regrets ("the fact that I left, etc.").
6. **ardorem:** "passion."

TWO POEMS OF UNKNOWN AUTHORSHIP: 1
([Tib.] 3.19 = 4.13)

The poet's love for his mistress.

1. **nobis:** dative of disadvantage after verb of depriving, *subducet*, "will steal." See on *Lygdamus* 1.27.
   lectum: i.e., "love."
2. **hoc...foedere:** emphatically placed; "It was on such terms...."
4. **oculis...meis:** dative of person (here "thing") judging, "in my eyes."
5. **uni:** i.e., *soli*.
   bella: See on *Lygdamus* 4.52.
7. **opus...est:** "there is need (of)" + ablative of separation.
   gloria: "boasting."
8. **qui sapit:** Take *ille* as antecedent.
   in...gaudeat...sinu: a proverbial expression, meaning to keep one's joys (which can excite envy and the evil eye) to oneself.
9. **ego:** emphatic, the poet contrasting himself with the *vulgus* (7).
10. **trita** < *tero*.
11-12. Understand *es* in all three parts of the tricolon.
11. **requies:** "respite."
13. **amica:** "girl-friend, mistress."
    Tibullo: dative of advantage; "for Tibullus." See Introduction.
14. **deficiet:** "will fail, be a failure."
    uenus: "love-making."
15. **tuae:** because Juno was a goddess especially concerned with and protective of women.
    iuro: here with two accusatives, the thing sworn (*hoc*) and the deity in whose name the oath is taken (*sancta...numina*). One normally expects *per* with the latter; see on *Lygdamus* 1.15.
17. **mea pignora:** "my guarantees, assurances" (sc. that the relationship would not be a "unequal" one).
18. **proderat:** "benefitted"; < *prosum*.
19. **fortis:** i.e., confident in my submission.
20. **peperit** < *pario*.
    misero: sc. *mihi*.
22. **notae:** i.e., to whom I am accustomed.
    seruitium: See on *Garland* 4.3.
23. **uinctus** < vincio: i.e., he is a *servus dominae suae* .

ad: "at." As a "slave" of love, the poet will, like maltreated real slaves, seek refuge at any altar, in his case that of Venus, the appropriate deity.
24. **notat iniustos:** "brands offenders" (i.e., those who are "unjust" in love).

TWO POEMS: 2
([Tib.] 3.20 = 4.14)

The girl rumoured to be unfaithful.

1. **peccare:** often used, in elegy, of infidelity.
2. **surdis auribus esse:** ablative of description or quality. Translate simply: "to be deaf."
3. **crimina:** "charges, accusations."
   nostro...dolore: with *sine*.
4. **miserum:** sc. *me*.